'Til the
STREETLIGHTS
Came On

For Jennifer

To A Classy
& elegant professional

All the Best

Jo

'Til the STREETLIGHTS Came On

LESSONS LEARNED

from

NEIGHBORHOOD GAMES

Daniel J. Porter

LANGDON STREET PRESS, MINNEAPOLIS

Langdon Street Press
212 3rd Avenue North, Suite 290
Minneapolis, MN 55401
612.455.2293
www.langdonstreetpress.com
Published in cooperation with TAPP House Publishing

ISBN-13: 978-1-938296-16-1
LCCN: 2012951009

Distributed by Itasca Books

Book Design by Mary Kristin Ross

All photographs © 2012 Barbara M. Porter. Used by permission

Printed in the United States of America

LANGDON
STREET PRESS

Dedicated in loving memory of my father
Thomas A. Porter
The Thundering Velvet Hand
The First Shirt
The Leader of the Band
for the wisdom you imparted
the dreams you inspired
the courage you instilled
and for your passionate belief that
the best is yet to be . . .

Acknowledgments

This book, a story reflecting on the blessings bestowed on me by the experiences of my youth, would not have been possible without the blessings I experience in my life today. I am surrounded and uplifted by the support of family, friends and colleagues to whom I am deeply grateful.

Inexpressible thanks and love to . . .

My wife Barbara, for all the hours of listening, brainstorming, sharing, editing, shooting the book's photos, single parenting, and talking me off my ledges, I thank you. For taking into your heart the dreams and aspirations of my heart, and for sacrificing to make them come true, I love you.

Our daughters, Chelsey and Karoline, who have not only endured more than their fair share of "when I was a kid" stories from their dad, they have also lent their spirit, love, and energy by proofing chapters, listening to speech excerpts, and collaborating on book design elements. You are amazing and I love you dearly.

Enduring thanks and love to . . .

My brothers, Tom, Kevin, and Tim—the Brothers Four. The gifts you have given my life through the experiences we shared gave me balance in direction in our youth and appreciation and love in our present day.

My sisters, Colleen, Cathy, Karen, and Eileen—guardians of heart matters and champions of my artistic efforts when we were young—kindred friends of heart as our family's journey continues to unfold.

My Mom—whose heart and mind and whose wit and wisdom shaped a view of life for her children that encouraged us to be resourceful, respectful, diligent, and devout, and to do so with humor and humility.

Special thanks to . . .

Finally, to the early readers and friends of this effort, my thanks go to: Jack Baranowski, Gary Beggs, Patrick Boyhan, Clay Buckley, Doug Buzenski, Mike Duvall, Anthony Gargiulo, Dave Kramer, Greg Maltby, Tony Nader, Rob Onorato, Jim Quintavalle, Sam Rutigliano, Ron Schmidt, Olivia Schwartz, Jim Smith, Russ Weaver, and Pat Winslow

Introduction

We shall never cease from exploration and the end of all our exploring will be to arrive where we started and know the place for the first time.

—T. S. Eliot

We played football in the street, from telephone pole to telephone pole, and counted first downs by the passes we completed. Our defensive schemes were built on counting five or seven "Mississippis" and included one "Mad-Dog" rush per four-down sequence.

We pieced together a baseball field from parts of each other's yards, and we called certain neighbor's yards "automatic outs" because of the ramifications sure to arise if an errant ball landed on their property.

We spent late-night summer hours dashing through darkened yards, across driveways, and in-between cars, all with the adrenaline rush of a covert rescue mission because we had to kick an empty coffee can and thus set our captive peers free.

We wiled away the hours on an eight-by-eight section of driveway with nothing but a ball and dozen variations of bouncing it in a game we called "four square." Freeze tag, T.V. tag, reverse tag, and body-part tag filled endless spring evenings and summer days.

If you did any of these, or something like them, chances are you are a part of the generation of American kids who grew up playing neighborhood games.

We grew up with what I might call "the best of nothing" . . . as in *no things*.

No microwaves, no dishwashers, no drink dispenser on the front of the refrigerator door. No cable, no satellite, and no recording devices to capture our favorite shows. No video games, no stereos, no phones that weren't physically connected to the wall. There were no organized activities beyond the school sports, which began in junior high for the select few who could compete well enough to earn the sparse spots. There were no mega sports stores to cater to every interest, and the only things open 24/7 were churches and hospitals.

Having none of these conveniences, resources, opportunities, or entertainments, we were sent outside in search of each other, in search of something to do. Once outside, having the best of nothing led us to having the best of everything by virtue of but one strategic approach we took to filling the void left by our circumstances.

We played.

We played from dawn till dusk and sometimes beyond. We played on our walkways and in our yards, on our driveways, and in the streets. We played any sport that was in season and any game that was within reason. And we did it all without any adult involvement, which is probably why it worked so well. I say it worked *well* . . . not perfectly. We fought, bickered, pouted, got over it, and played some more. We were a self-correcting bunch because the love of playing drove us to overcome the vicissitudes of our behavior.

We were the generation who grew up playing "sandlot ball." That's what my father used to call it. A moniker associated with neighborhood play from a time when the playing field of an inner-city neighborhood was quite literally a vacant sandlot. We appropriated the term for our games of choice because it sounded infinitely better than to say we were playing tag, hide-and-seek, or wiffle ball.

Time and tide has changed our culture, and many of us will wax poetic the days of our youth. But in the enumeration of embellished feats, I think we forget to notice how deeply our experiences shaped our approach to our adult lives.

As an adult, I have been blessed to realize my life's dream of becoming a published author (I have published twenty-two books for children and young adults on themes ranging from stress management and character building to Internet mystery adventures and non-fiction educational resources) and am even more fortunate to be the invited guest speaker for corporate events, school graduations, and organizational dinners—yet, absent the lessons learned from neighborhood games, I would have accomplished none of these things.

I was born with dystonia, the nation's third most common muscle movement disorder. Described succinctly, dystonia is the involuntary movement of voluntary muscles. If you reflect on that description just a moment longer . . . *the involuntary movement of voluntary muscles* . . . you will find within those words, as I have, a recipe for sports adventure. It essentially means the two activities you never want to engage in with me are: golf and . . . darts. I cannot be held responsible for what happens. (I say that with all due and dear deference to those suffering with dystonia; self-depreciating humor has always been the balm I have applied to the sores left by the disease.)

My dystonia is classified as "multifocal dystonia" because two or more of my body areas are impacted by the disease. There are four major presentations of the disease and for the one and only time in my life—I hit for the cycle—I have all four. I have cervical—affecting the muscles around the neck, causing twitching and spasmodic movement of the head; oromandibular—causing distortions of the mouth and tongue; and focal hand, or "writer's cramp dystonia," which causes spastic movements of the hands. But perhaps the most pronounced and easily recognizable form my dystonia takes is called "spasmodic dysphonia," which reduces my vocal quality to a horse, halting whisper so that it sounds like I am choking or running out of breath as I endeavor to speak.

My disease wasn't formally diagnosed until I was thirteen; so, for much of my childhood, I was thought of as a nervous, anxious child with a speech impediment so profound that I rarely spoke in class. As for the disease's effects on my physical coordination—let's just say I was not the "go-to guy" on third and long. Because of the disease I didn't walk well until the age of three, didn't master riding a bike until I was ten, and swallowed answers to questions in class for fear of the ridicule I believed would ensue whenever I spoke aloud.

Given the presence of this silent, and at that time unidentified, prankster in the days of my childhood, the circumstances of my family life could not have been a more well-designed and powerful elixir for my spirit. When you are born the seventh of eight children, you had better learn to speak at home, or, likely as not, you're going to be hungry. My family, through their normal daily movements, imbued with their rapier-sharp Irish wit and evidenced by their staunch defense and support, infused in me a love of life and a passion to be part of all I saw unfolding around me. There was no sulking in one's room, no enabling to be less than I could be. In the home of my youth it was "all-up-and-all-in"—not by parental mandate, but by the passionate pursuit of living a full life.

I was in my early twenties when I began to fully come to terms with the disease I tried to deny existed in me, even after it was diagnosed. I went back to the children's hospitals I had spent so much time in and retraced the evolution of the medical testing that had yielded dystonia as the diagnosis of my disease. I met with the doctors who had overseen my case and they opened the medical records for me. I found in one medical chart a doctor's note that forever underscored the tonic my family applied to my disease. It read:

"Amiable young boy with great familial and community

support. His insatiable zeal to keep up with his older brothers may indeed alter the course of his disease. Clearly, it has altered his orientation to it."

For me, there could be no more compelling nor clear evidence of the value of playing neighborhood games than to say: I wouldn't be who I am today had it not been for the hours of strengthening, stretching, resistance training, and spirit-aerobics otherwise disguised as tackle football in the side yard, stick ball in the street, and ghosts-in-the-graveyard in the field behind my best friend's house.

I have come to believe the enduring legacy of the sandlot was the way in which it inspired us to be a true community. We were so heavily and richly invested in one another. We needed each other. In turn, we inspired, mentored, cajoled, motivated, admonished, tolerated, and celebrated one another. Older kids taught younger kids, and younger kids passed the lessons on to their successors. We covered for each other, pulled each other up, or brought each other back down to earth.

My childhood friends shaped so much of my approach to friendships, to challenges, to conflicts, and *to* life—and yet I never recall having a single conversation with them *about* life.

Through the periods of reflection, which gave rise to writing this book, I have been humbled, awed, and amazed at the vast number of people to whom I am indebted for the legacy laden gifts their lives have given to mine. I look at my life differently as a result of looking at my past differently. I have come to believe we are each setting about making a mosaic, a tapestry, a pointillist painting, but we can only get our art supplies from one another. Through our exchanges, we trade the colors, tiles, and threads we weave into the fabric of our lives.

I think of all my experiences in the neighborhoods as giving me a never-ending cache of art supplies I can contribute to the works of art who are the people I live with, encounter, or befriend in my life. Any insight shared, any moment of respite, any cause for celebration I can give another is the legacy I hope to leave in honor of all that has been given to me.

I began to think it important to bring forward a sampling of the experiences we shared as a generation growing up at play in our neighborhoods. I wanted to leave a journal, a trail marker for future generations, something that speaks to the truths, joys, and riches lavished upon so many of us who experienced the riches of neighborhood games.

So this work has emerged, with my thanks to all those who contributed to it, not as a comparison to the activities of today's youth, but as a collection of cherished memories, experiences, and life-shaping insights harvested from countless hours of participating in neighborhood games.

If the telling of these stories awakens memories of your own, or sends you in search of someone who can share theirs, I am pleased. If the reading of these accounts inspires you to pass on the gems of your childhood, then I have succeeded in awakening the great wealth locked within the moments we spent playing. . . *'til the streetlights came on.*

Daniel J. Porter
Chagrin Falls, Ohio

Table of Contents

Participate

As the Screen Door Swings

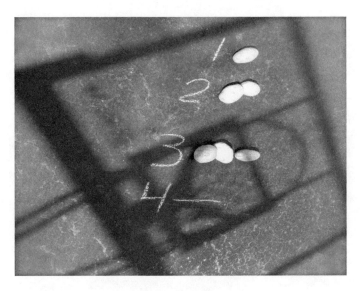

Put Your Potatoes In

The Playing Field is Never Level

Participate

*Such happiness as life is capable of, only comes
from full participation in it.*
—*John Dewey*

It was as simple as it was pristine. It was immutable. It could not be altered nor compromised in any way. The first law of neighborhood games I can remember internalizing, the law upon which the entire neighborhood universe rested was this: if you wanted to be *in*, you needed to be *out*. To be considered part of the in crowd among a group of your schoolmates was always a conditional proposition at best; to be considered part of the in crowd among your neighborhood mates was as easy as stepping outside and being ready to play.

Participate. Contribute. Be available. That was the deal you signed up for the day your parents moved into a neighborhood. No one had to text you, no cell phones rang, and the rotary phone on the wall didn't have speed dial. But there was no need. There was a sophisticated network of communication in place—your friends *expected* you to be out.

It wasn't *peer pressure* as much as it was *peer pleasure*. If you were a kid growing up in America in our generation (1950–1980), it didn't take you long to learn that if you wanted to have fun, fun was outside. Parents reinforced this notion quite efficiently with a simple, immutable law of their own: if you were home, you were available for chores.

As an adult, I attend coaching clinics where a great deal of time is spent teaching us how to protect, recognize, or honor a child's self-esteem. We are cautioned not to emphasize *winning* because children should be exalted for *trying*.

Kids playing in our neighborhood got that right away.

Sure, we all wanted to win, but as much as winning was momentarily coveted, the goal was always, first and foremost, to play. I think we lost something when outdoor neighborhood play disappeared. We started asking, even demanding, that organized activities replace, for our children, the sense of fulfillment we knew from participating in unstructured, unsupervised, peer-to-peer interaction. While there were many dreamers among us, deep down we knew the experiences we were getting in each other's backyard or the streets in front of our homes were as close as we were going to get to the real thing. Far from feeling faux, those experiences were the oxygen of our athletic self-esteem.

By the sheer volume of hours we invested in play, we were afforded the chance to be the hero; the one to hit the winning jumper; to "touch 'em all" on a walk-off grand slam; to kick the can that set everyone free.

I don't know of anyone who played in neighborhood games who didn't, at some point, get to experience the exhilaration of a peak performance—that moment when you surprised yourself and everyone else by making *the play*. The adulation of our peers and their unmitigated excitement memorialized the epic nature of our accomplishments and created talisman moments that instantly became the stuff of neighborhood lore.

"Remember when Kenny dove for that fly ball, caught it, and it landed on the hood of the car that was turning down Carson Street?"

"And remember when Andy caught that Hail Mary pass from Chuck—then had to immediately hurdle the fire hydrant, but missed and cracked his skull open?"

If by chance you flubbed your moment of glory, if you missed the winning shot or stubbed your toe on the clutch play, your shot at redemption was as close as the next game played, which usually came that day, or at worst, the next day when the gathering ritual again summoned everyone from their homes.

The gathering ritual was like watching ducks enter a pond. The first one in usually pulled the others in behind. In our neighborhood I was usually the first one out the door. In fact, the only time I ever heard the phrase, "Can Dan come out to play?" was when I couldn't, owing to some chores or grounding for failing to do said chores.

Once out, I headed for Donny Marshall's house. Donny and I would go call out Billy and Kenny. It wouldn't be long before our sounds in the streets would summon Chuckie, Ty, and Bobby—and with our ducks in a row, the games began.

If we were looking to play coed, my sister Eileen was the lynchpin; if Eileen showed, we were assured of getting Lisa, Kaye, and Michelle to play. You always had those "heavy hitters," the atoms of our neighborhood universe that could pull in so many others by virtue of their presence. They were the ones who ensured we'd have the critical mass we needed to play.

I've never again experienced the sustained personal affirmation that neighborhood play gave me. Rarely, if ever, does your mere physical presence add such energy and excitement to a group or event as it did when you would step from your home and represent another player for the game, or the player that made another type of game possible. You haven't lived until you've heard a group of your friends chant your name with unabashed enthusiasm because they knew you represented the key that unlocked the gates to the fields of play.

In the sports and playground games universe of school, not only was I often overlooked—let's just say the times I did come into view were not all that affirming. The balm to my young soul came when the guys in the neighborhood saw me coming, knew it meant our games were about to begin, and let loose with chants of "Dan-nee, Dan-nee, Dan-nee . . ."

Participation in the neighborhood offered you the joy of being part of something with no strings attached. It was an extended family of sorts, where you were accepted unconditionally because your presence filled a spot only you could fill. Modern life has a tendency to apply structure to the unstructured things of our youth; but I dare say "organized everything" can't give you the sense of abandon and whimsy our neighborhood games gave us.

I shudder to think of the feats of athleticism I would have missed if "organized everything" had been the order of our day. We had a guy in our neighborhood who possessed the sweetest swing of a bat you ever saw. He was pure poetry in motion. He knew how to strike the "power hitter's pose." That's the one where the batter rips through a pitch and then, at right about the three-quarter mark of his arc, he lets go and finishes the swing with one hand. This guy was our Sultan of Swat, our King of Swing. Every time he came up to bat, we shifted the outfield four blocks north.

We all went to see him play his Pony League games. We wanted to be on hand for the birth of his legend, to see others discover what we had witnessed ourselves in our neighborhood.

He never hit a ball out of the infield.

That's one of the problems with organized everything . . . you don't get to be the hero very often. You don't get to stretch the limits of your imagination when the home run fence really *is* three hundred feet to "straight away center."

Neighborhood play was also a respite from cultural chronological stigmas. If you were an eighth grader, chances were your play at school bore no resemblance to your play at home. You could run around your neighborhood with reckless, childlike abandon, playing games with kids four to six years younger than you without any repercussions. It was always *Never Land* in your neighborhood.

Come to think of it, eighth grade was *the career year* for

those of us who played neighborhood games. Usually we had grown to a level of physical maturity whereby we were good enough to be a meaningful player in most games, and yet, we were young enough that no one looked askance at us for *playing* in those games.

Ninth graders would still play neighborhood games, but they'd be looking over their shoulders all the time to make sure no one saw them playing.

Tenth graders still wanted to play but didn't.

Juniors would consent to play if they thought it would embellish their status as legends among the young, aspiring sandlotters of the hood.

Seniors . . . they wanted to be adults.

Adults . . . they wanted to be eighth graders.

We learned so many things by virtue of our participation and our availability to the rhythms and subtleties of our world.

We learned you really can fry an egg on the sidewalk in the heat of mid-July sun. We learned what dew smells like as it evaporates quickly on a late August morning. We learned how to pick up the hint of an approaching storm front or a harbinger of autumn coming on a suddenly crisp breeze during a September afternoon. We learned how warm you could feel inside a fort you built into a snow bank.

I know kids of today experience these things; I just think we had a more poignant relationship to them. It's different from the seat of your English Racer than it is from the back of an SUV.

We also *heard* our world differently as kids.

When I started thinking more deeply than the idle conversations which inevitably begin with "When we were kids . . ." the first conscious thought I had was the realization of this most rudimentary sensory level difference—we heard our world differently than kids do today.

Be it caused by our ever-advancing technologies, our

thirst for convenience, or our defensive reaction to the rising tide of insanity in the interactions of our society, we seem to have moved steadily into a state of isolation wherein the world around us is muted and we filter in that to which we choose to listen.

But it wasn't always so.

For most of us growing up in the 1950s, '60s, and the better part of the '70s, whole-house air conditioning meant that your mom opened every window in the *whole house* the first warm day of spring and didn't close them again until the first chilly evening in the fall. (Those who can remember the burnt metal smell of a screen after it had baked all day in the August heat, will know what I speak.) Through those open windows of our homes, the ambient noises of our world beckoned us, calling out the cadence of our days.

I remember watching westerns and war movies with my dad on Saturday nights (a practice driven less by any notion of familial bonding than by the fact there was only one T.V. in the house; however, the ideal of the former was well served by the reality of the latter). The characters who always drew my awe were the trappers, the guides, and the frontiersmen. The guys who were so in tune with their world they knew what every movement, every change in the wind, every sound meant. Like Daniel Boone and his sidekick, Mingo.

If Old Dan'l heard a branch snap in the distance—he could tell you the weight of the animal "what stepped on it." If he detected a change in the wind, he'd give you a ten-day forecast around which you could plan a wedding. Then there was Mingo. Mingo, the Oxford-educated Native American who could quote Shakespeare, and yet still gently run his fingers through a track mark and tell you what the animal ate for breakfast (at least I think it was the track mark he was feeling). To me, there was something so cool, in a primal sort of way, about having that kind of awareness and knowledge of your world.

Thinking of it now, that's exactly how we were as kids. What Old Dan'l and Mingo knew about their backwoods, we knew about our neighborhoods.

Take a typical summer day. From the moment we woke, we could lie in our beds and hear the pregame countdown begin because when your playing field included some, or all, of the streets that ran through your neighborhood, you learned every possible factor that could affect your play.

6:30 a.m.: The thud of the paper on the front porch—two hours until "game time." (It took until 8:30 for the morning commute traffic to clear our streets, which would then remain virtually car-free until 4:30 that afternoon.)

7:00 a.m.: The gurgle of your family's coffee pot churning out its black gold—ninety minutes until game time.

7:30 a.m.: The roar of Mr. Pruschetti's Plymouth wagon . . . T-Minus sixty minutes and counting.

Cued by this melliferous morning melee, we headed down for a bowl of frosted something-or-others and listened for a signal from which we drew further indications of what the day held in store.

Our communication network was closer to the beating of tribal drums than today's web of technology. We moved to the sounds of our world with sublime synchronicity. Noises that seemed inconsequential to others were Morse code to our awaiting ears. We simply listened to the world around us— and we knew what to do.

A tennis ball bouncing off the Paressis' garage meant we'd be heading to the park for our version of grand slam tennis— which was actually more like dodge ball than serve and volley.

The sound of a baseball card in the spokes of Chad Altwerth's Stingray told us to grab our towels, tell our moms we'd be home by dinner, see if we could score a buck or two, and head to the city pool for the day.

Rocks against the stop sign equaled baseball at the corners of McLaughlin and North Broadway. The clank of a shot off a loose rim was a call to order in the Finnerans' driveway for a game of hoops. And the sound an over-inflated football makes when you punt it may as well have been an air horn signaling the start of the race—we heard that and we headed for Edison Field where our epic gridiron battles unfolded.

The end of the day was much the same. I don't remember any of us being particularly mechanically inclined, but all of us could tell you—just by listening to the sound of the engine (or muffler, as it were)—who was coming and going in the neighborhood and what it meant to our game. Volkswagen Beetles and Buses? Please, those were easy. We were so good we could tell an Olds 98 from a Buick LeSabre. We could hear the low rolling rumble of a Chevy wagon with a bad muffler, tell you how many blocks away it was, and if there was time enough for one more at bat. We knew whose car signaled the two-minute warning and whose meant sudden-death overtime.

But of all the auditory harbingers of our days, to me the most reliable and distinguishable were our screen doors.

As the Screen Door Swings

Hearing and heading the call to participate

Many of the neighborhoods we lived in were housing developments of the post-WWII era. Row houses set back an equal distance from the street and separated by identical-width driveways. When the windows were open, a sound tunnel of sorts was formed and you could hear a screen door open ten houses away.

Most of us had the wood-framed variety, which were basically screens stretched across a one-by-two frame with tightly coiled springs on the crossbar. The ones that sounded like cats screeching when we opened them, and then closed with a signature ***thwap!*** To be sure, as the cruel march of time went on, some of our more well-to-do compadres saw their homes outfitted with aluminum-framed screen doors with their springs encased in a "quiet-close" gas cylinder, but a well-trained ear could still pick up the *whoosh* of their movements, or the sound of their metal chains bouncing up against their aluminum frame.

I made my judgment of who was coming out to play by the time in between the stretching of the spring . . . and the *thwap* of the door closing. For example, Billy Yurich lived three houses away, but I always knew when he was coming out to play because the spring on his screen door was hyper, frenetic, and immediate . . . like Billy.

His whole coming-out-to-play sequence was like a radio

11

play-by-play man calling a home run. There was the high-pitched, gleeful exclamation of the spring opening the door. *"Back, back, back she goes . . ."* and the immediate thwapping of the door closing behind him. *"Gone!"* Moments later Billy arrived in our driveway.

Donny Marshall lived catty-corner to our house, a deep center-field-to-home-plate throw away, and still I always knew when he was coming out to play. Donny's spring screen door had a far more pragmatic sound than Billy's. It was like its owner, as well. It released the same number of synchronized moans because Donny opened it the same distance each time. It was unequivocal as it closed with its decisive baritone thud because Donny released it at the same point every time. Indeed, it was consistent, accurate, and unflappable, like Donny. And never in a hurry; you couldn't rush Donny with an All-Pro NFL lineman.

The screen door of our house?

No one could ever tell you what it sounded like because there is not a person alive who knows.

My three brothers and I were like ninjas when we exited the house in search of play. We were making ourselves candidates for Special Forces training. We'd just . . . disappear. In a home filled with eight children, you could pretty well figure there'd always be a chore awaiting completion, so announcing you were going out to play was never advisable. My father hated noises born of low maintenance. He once told me he never had a home with a creaky hinge or squeaky spring.

We listened intently to our world. Not because we had reached some pinnacle of wisdom; rather, it was because we had no choice. We didn't have earphones to jam in our ears at all times. Our playgrounds weren't virtual. There was usually only one TV in the house and daytime programming left much to be desired; FM radio was still trying to find its way; and you had to ask permission to use the family stereo. So, in the absence of electronic interference, we listened to the world around us.

What we heard shaped what we did; and what we did shaped who we became.

This interaction with the real-time movements of our environments broadened our understanding of what it takes to adapt, adjust, sacrifice, and compromise in the pursuit of our dreams, even if they were only dreams of greatness on our fields of play.

Imagine for a moment we had scrawled messages in the dirt of our childhood playing fields. Suppose we had the foresight to summarize our experiences and pass down their wisdom to the generations that followed us. I often go back in my mind to remember what we knew then—and I've brought some of those messages forward in these short free-verse poems I call *Sand Scripts*.

Sand Scripts

You are a part of your environment
as much as your environment is part of you.
Take time to be in it.
To watch it.
To listen to it.
To learn the lessons
only it can give you.
Hear and heed its call
to participate.

Put Your Potatoes In

Making the commitment to participate

On this one point, I believe, modern life has completely missed it.

Our current culture relies on *talking* behaviors, such as responsibility, reliability, and dependability, into children. In our day, *experiences* created the behaviors that formed our characters. To be sure, we heard our parents speak to these values, and their discipline around them was *very* exacting; but, there were no parents in, near, by, at, or presiding over our "play groups." What made the application of these core values take root for us was our friends. We taught one another to share, to play fair, and to be dependable. It was a peer-to-peer behavior modification program at its finest.

Your friends would not hesitate to crack you in the back of the head, put you in line, or "coach you up" if your behavior was less than acceptable. In the world of neighborhood games, there was too much riding on each person's participation to allow anyone to be less than responsible, or reliable. To the notion of having a willingness to participate, we added a crucial ingredient—it was the *commitment* to participate. Or, as we simply called it, *"Put your potatoes in."*

Think about it. How great a phrase is that?

"Put your potatoes in."

Granted, at face value it seems like an odd phrase, almost

like an ante call in a poker game at a farmer's market, but upon closer examination, it's really a fascinating incantation fraught with meaning and consequence. Indeed, one would be hard pressed to find a better phrase in modern lexicon. To fully understand the intrinsic genius of the phrase, one must understand what it meant to maintaining the attributes of randomness, chance, and variability in our neighborhood games.

Responding to the call to "put your potatoes in" meant standing with feet shoulder length apart, arms extended, hands balled into a fist, and presented into a common circle. I submit to you there is no way to maintain one's cool, one's swagger, or one's "street cred" while standing in just such a pose. I remember older kids partaking in this sacred selection rite, all the while looking around the neighborhood like an informant talking to an undercover cop. They were hoping no one would see their potatoes. Why? Because we were vulnerable; we were exposed; we were committed.

With this single action, what we were essentially saying was, "I'm in. You can count on me to participate no matter the team I'm on or the role I'm given. I'm part of this activity and there's no going back."

With everyone committed to the process, the canter started the chant. "One potato/two potato/three potato/four . . ."

With each word the canter tapped the participant's potato with his own potato, "five potato/six potato/seven potato/ more."

You had to say "more" to rhyme with "four" and keep the universal energy flowing in harmony, balance, and rhythm. It was a kind of a selection feng shui.

As random and equitable a process as it seems, it was not without attempts to influence the hand of fate.

In some neighborhoods you could add to the count chant. "One potato/two potato/three potato four/five potato six potato/seven potato/more—and you are not it/not because you're dirty/not because you're clean/just because you kiss the boys behind the magazines . . ."

Then there was the syllabic shift—you could go traditional and count "you are" as two beats depending on whom it was going to land on, or you could slur it into the contraction "you're" and have it fall to *your* favor.

It also depended on the chant of choice. With all our fists thrust into the circle of participation, the cantor could choose any number of chants. A fan favorite in our neighborhood was "Inka Bink a bottle of ink/the cork fell off/and now you stink." Not to be outdone by "Bubble gum bubble gum in a dish/how many pieces do you wish?"

In really serious neighborhoods it was "My mother punched your mother in the nose/what color blood came out?"

The great equalizer was the post-chant addendum "and you are not it/not because you're tall/not because you're small/ but because no one wants you at all."

We had a kid in our neighborhood who had an abacus-like mind. His name was Kenny Strankowski. If he wanted you on his team, Kenny would be whispering in your ear as the count chant unfolded. "Say purple" he'd tell you if you were asked the color of your mother's nasal hemorrhage. He'd tell you the exact number of bubblegum pieces to request, the exact place to stand in line depending on where the count commenced.

It worked for everyone but me. I listened to everything Kenny told me and yet, I never ended up on his team. . . .

Reflecting on all the angst over how every act in modern life is taken as being a "statement about" or "action against" our personhood leads me to wonder how we ever pulled off the often isolating team selection processes we used as kids.

What did we understand then that we have lost sight of now?

I think we understood that we couldn't manipulate outcomes before we participated. I've seen it too many times where parents will pull a child from one team and spare no expense to place them on another team—so they can have the best possible outcome.

You know how we ensured the best possible outcome?

We played our hearts out. We tried our best, often against the odds, and left it all on the field of play.

And do you know what the best possible outcome of that was?

The fact that we played our hearts out.

We understood attendance was not the same as participation. Attendance was showing up; participation was contributing. We understood our neighborhood universe, like life, often dealt us a random set of consequences, and we had to do our best to eke joy and accomplishment out of them. We didn't seek a statistically probable outcome—we sought the chance to play and we were willing to be vulnerable to do so.

We put our potatoes in.

Sand Scripts

If your participation
in something, doesn't, at some level
make you vulnerable . . .
it isn't going to
produce anything
you will
cherish.

The Playing Field Is Never Level

Taking yourself too seriously—can take you out of the game

There is a world of difference between creating equal *access to* our fields of play and creating equal *experiences from* our fields of play. Modern life tries to make these two attributes equal for every child who ever picks up a ball or enters a contest. They never have been; they never will be; nor should they ever be.

I make this assertion as someone who lived on what many would view the "short end of the stick" when it comes to access to equal experiences from games of skill or competitions of physical competency. And yet, I will tell you, as I tell most anyone who will listen, the greatest thing that *never* happened to me was that I was never accommodated. The bar was set where the bar was set; the playing field was *never* level, and this timeless truth saved my life.

I was born the seventh of eight children: four boys and four girls. Our family moved quite a bit as my father's career advanced, but every place we went we were greeted with open arms simply because we doubled the neighborhood play rosters. (Some would say a family with eight children *is* a neighborhood, but that's another story.) I had two older brothers who were each bona fide all-state athletes in track and basketball, respectively, and two of my four older sisters could play sports with anyone. No one had to lobby for gender equality in our neighborhoods. If you could fill a spot or play a role, you were chosen. (We won't even discuss how many times my sisters were selected for roster spots before me.)

Our family had a proud lineage of athleticism . . . and then there was me.

Because of my dystonia, my muscles either abduct, which is to move the limb away from the body, or adduct, which is to move the limb toward the body. This biological fact was entirely dismissed by my brothers and never dissuaded them from expecting me to participate in the games of the season. So, when it came time to learn how to play golf, my brothers took me to the driving range, and as I began experiencing a different muscle spasm with each swing, my brothers' conversations went something like this:

"Wow, that's the most vicious slice I've ever seen."

"Check that, he's got one nasty hook."

"I don't think I've ever seen a golf ball do that before."

"Hey, let's have him play hockey—that should be interesting!"

I received an enormous gift as a child: my family taught me not to take myself too seriously—because to take yourself too seriously is to take yourself out of the game.

Despite my infirmities, my physical limitations, I was totally accepted in every neighborhood we lived in (which for me had been five different neighborhoods in ten years) because I could participate in the games. I endured the occasional wisecrack that came my way referencing my condition, but every kid in the neighborhood got cracked on in one way or another. Life was mainstreaming me. I was learning that to be part of something meant you had to participate, even if you weren't the best or even if you might look silly trying. That realization alone was a glorious liberation from the effects of my disease.

Most kids crave the sense of inclusion; life in our neighborhoods never failed to provide that for me. I always found my self-esteem was safe among my neighborhood friends. School—not so much, but it was all good in the 'hood. Maybe it was due in part from the knowledge that "we better keep Danny coming back if we want a fourth for our games," but I also believe more than a fair amount of it was owed to an underlying generosity of spirit kids seem to universally possess.

It *is* true that until I was nine, I thought a "spaz" was actually a position on a football team. My brothers would need another player and someone would say, "get the spaz . . ." and they would call for me. I would trot out onto the field to the (imagined) adulation of the throngs and masses, like a reliever being summoned from the bullpen. Still, it was a small price to pay for feeling I was part of the group. I was the coveted second, third, or fourth guy who made the games possible. I had an unquestioned, unshaken sense of belonging.

Had there been accommodations made for me, had someone sought to "level the playing field" by allowing me six strikes, not three, or instructed my fellow players to go soft and let me catch the "third and short" pass, had they purposely slowed so I could catch them when I was "it," for me the results would have been devastating. I'm not suggesting all such accommodations are ill conceived. Indeed, they can be ennobling and appropriate in many cases. My contention is that modern culture seems to be seeking to invoke them in *every case*, whether a physical challenge is present or not.

Participating—that was the accommodation, and we gave it freely in our neighborhood games. We learned that no matter how badly we had been bullied, overlooked, mistreated, or made to feel inferior at school, a few moments of play in our neighborhood could reset our internal compass to due north. Neighborhood games were the safest incubator a kid could ever know. It was there where it was okay to fail untold dozens of times. I can't imagine the thousands of times my brothers threw footballs, baseballs, and basketballs to me. I can't fathom the number of miles we ran playing tag. I *can* tell you how much they impacted me. They allowed me to develop skills that would have remained undeveloped in any other environment.

One of the problems in our world of "organized everything" is that kids are constantly on display. We cart them off to organized sports and activities where access to skill building diminishes by the number of kids on the team and the amount of time for the "practice." We practiced four to six hours a day . . . but we called it *play*.

Our modern process breeds self-consciousness. For starters, there's always an adult or two present to coach and supervise. And since "organized everything" always has a performance, as parents we see our children's physical development out of context. We see every undeveloped skill a child has, and they immediately become an issue, a cause for concern. I can tell you for certain that if I had been born in this generation, I would not have developed as much as I was blessed to develop. Why? I would have been too self-conscious of my limitations and I would have recoiled from the process.

My father had a very simple philosophy and response when any of the eight of us would decry a situation that was not "fair." He would look at you with an expression of such resolve that you knew there was no sense in pleading your case as he would say, "You'll find 'sympathy' in the dictionary after 'shit' because it's worth less than that."

My family and friends had a great coping strategy, as well—it was called *humor*. Their love of laughing, endless repartee, and equal opportunity roasting taught me not to take myself too seriously. My older brother was fond of dropping into his best *Foghorn Leghorn* voice and saying of me:

"That boy couldn't catch a cold."

"Danny? Danny threw the ball in the air one time—and *missed*."

"I say, I say, watching that boy run is like watching an

ostrich try to walk on hot coals."

There are only now, thirty years later, starting to be medicines that affect dystonia. My medicine was our neighborhood games. Because of my level of activity and my participation in thousands of hours of neighborhood play, my strength and coordination improved to a point that began to mitigate the effects of the muscle movement disorder. I went on to play competitive basketball in high school; today, I run marathons and have a motivational speaking career. When people ask me what drove me to overcome the effects of my disease, I have a simple response:

I never set out to overcome my multifocal dystonia. I just wanted to play.

And I thank God and my family that the playing field was never level.

Sand Scripts

Only after I had
scaled the summit of my dreams
did I realize the value
of the burdens I had carried
over the rocky paths
of my journey—
they had made my legs
strong enough
for the climb.

Contribute

Be the Fire Hydrant

Occasionally, You Gotta Serve Up a Tater

Of Moon Pies, Mallow Bars, & Mrs. Price

Contribute

It is not what we take up,
but what we give up,
that makes us rich.
—Henry Ward Beecher

In many ways our neighborhoods were like ensemble theater troupes whose characters knew each other so well they improvised entire three-act plays on a moment's notice. Everyone's contribution was vital and valuable because, while it was participation that made the games possible, it was our contribution that made the games the irreplaceable staple of our existence, and now of our memories.

For some of us, the contribution was to provide the bats, the bases, the ball, or the playing field. For others, it was to fill a spot on the roster and thus even out the teams. For others still, the contribution was to round up the treats we enjoyed after the game (in every neighborhood there was a go-to treat kid, the one whose mother flew in the face of convention by offering sugar snacks irrespective of the time of day, what you ate for lunch, or even if you were allowed to partake). Regardless of the role, everyone understood that the entire system relied on each of us playing our part, each of us making a contribution.

At times it was tough to bow to the mores of the moment—like when you got a brand new baseball for your birthday. I can remember opening the box and holding it up to my nose just to smell the rawhide, like a wine connoisseur. Smelling it first was the proper protocol; it would have been gouache to just grab it out of the box. Next, I would reach in and gently remove it, as though I was a diamond thief trying not to trip the alarm. At this point the proper technique was to rotate it with the fingers of one hand, tossing it lightly in the air as if to check its weight and balance. I was like Indiana Jones looking at a lost treasure. I wanted that ball to stay new forever, even though I knew it wouldn't. I wanted to place it like a trophy on my dresser, even though I knew the code of the day was to bring it out to play.

I'd die at the first scuff mark or grass stain on its white rawhide and never blink at the second one. The first popped stitch was a tragedy, the rest became folklore.

It was the same for footballs. Nothing like holding one so new you could still feel the little leather beads the manufacturer put in for grip. The only thing that compared to it was holding the same ball when the leather was smooth enough to roll cookie dough with it, or when the laces were so worn the bladder was coming through them. When you visit our homes in our adulthood, it is the worn-smooth footballs and the "letters knocked off of them" baseballs you'll find along the bookcases and trophy ledges in our finished basements.

It was a marvelously self-regulating universe as I recall it. We learned to involve everyone to a level that made sense for the game. It was always about *the game*. You got your breaks when the circumstances allowed, not due to any notion of entitlement. If all you could throw was a fit, you were not going to play quarterback. If you had stones for hands, you could count on blocking the line. If you were slower than a sermon on a summer Sunday, you could count on playing an attending role, not a primary one.

The neighborhood ecosystem for players was iron clad. It was intuitive and we knew how it worked. On those days when not many kids were around, everyone played and, to a large degree, everyone got their shot at the glory positions. As the number of participants increased, the key roles went to the best players. De facto, no negotiation involved. Sometimes the rosters for games were filled, and the lost and unchosen were left to fill their own time their own way—it's just the way it was. You couldn't go home because you were risking chores, and if you told your parents you hadn't been chosen to play— well, that was an untenable solution, as well.

For me, I knew if Chad Altwerth was around to fill out the sixth spot for a three-on-three-because-six-players-are-all-that-fit-on-the-court, I knew I could plan on practicing my Acorn Toss. Acorn Toss is a little known game of skill. It was invented to pass the time spent on sidelines and involved tossing acorns through the lattice fence that bordered Mrs. Wilson's yard. I am certain if I were to return there today, there'd be a forest where once she proudly displayed her rose garden.

The power of these neighborhood mores—that you made the contribution circumstances called upon you to make— began for me my very first day of neighborhood play— and has remained a stanchion of my life to this day. It can be summed up to say: your role was your contribution and your contribution was your role. If you took that relationship seriously, both expanded. For me, it all began with a fire hydrant.

Be the Fire Hydrant

Your role in the play . . . is to play your role

I remember the first day I was called up to the "bigs." I was sitting on the second stoop of our front yard. Our home, at the time, sat upon a short hill that separated our wrap-around front porch from the slate sidewalks of the day. To bridge the expanse of thirty feet, the builders constructed two flights of six steps each, with a landing in between. Short stone walls kept the integrity of the design; my favorite thing to do was to sit on the downward slope of the second stoop. When you are six years old, sitting on a downward sloping edifice a mere twelve feet from traffic qualified as death defying. I was sitting there, trying to stack fallen buckeyes into a 3-D pyramid, when my older brothers "sprung" me from the prison sentence endured by those youth confined to the boundaries of their yard.

I found out years later that their generosity to include me that day had been born of a maternal mandate ("Take Danny with you") and intoned with my father's assurance that I would be well looked after (". . . and know this, what happens to *him* happens to *you*") Here I had this patriarchal dispensation and didn't even know it. Whatever the case, I was on my way to the vaunted sandlot of the time—*Edison Field*.

Professional sports have their storied and hallowed venues of play.

Lambeau Field.

The Polo Grounds.

"The House That Ruth Built"—Yankee Stadium

Madison Garden.

For us, it was Edison Field. A moniker still whispered to this day to give it the reverence it deserves. It was called Edison Field because it was a patch of unused land adjacent to the parking lot of the Ohio Edison Electric Company's substation in our neighborhood. Hallowed fields of play are never so because of their physical attributes; rather, their legends come from the legions that played upon them.

The fact that you couldn't see Edison Field from the street only added to its stature. I remember many a fall weekend watching my brothers disappear up the winding drive, only to vanish around a final turn of that asphalt runway to glory. I would watch them like Ray Kinsella watching Shoeless Joe Jackson disappear into the cornfield in *Field of Dreams*. And now, acres of azure blue skies above, the maples, elms, ash, and sycamores adorned in a mid-fall Mardi Gras of color, the air fresh and crisp—I laid foot to path and made my first ascent to Edison Field.

The physical exertion needed to arrive at the edge of Edison Field only added to the exhilaration of the moment. Making the turn that always took the view of my brothers from me opened my first view of our storied sandlot.

It was in a natural hollow of the land, formed by slight hills that rose up from the backs of each end zone. The eastern sideline was marked by a row of towering white pines. The western sideline was formed by a gravel parking area off the asphalt of the entrance road. Another storied element of Edison Field was the vineyard you could get to through the arbor on the southwest corner of the end zone. I remember having the good sense to gasp upon my first view of Edison Field, a reaction approved of by my older brothers. Of all the sandlots in all the world, ours was epic indeed, and neophytes should display the proper amount of reverence, awe, and amazement.

Tom, my eldest brother, my childhood hero, and my sandlot mentor, convinced me to play a key, pivotal role that day. First he gave me the lay of the land.

"Okay, the pine trees are out of bounds on that side of the field; the rocks are out of bounds on this side. These two big trees mark the end zone on this end of the field. You know what an end zone is, right?"

I nodded frantically in the affirmative.

"Okay then, Danny . . ." Tom inserted a pregnant pause like a commander about to ask a subordinate to take on a dangerous mission, ". . . I need you to do something for me."

Picture a Norman Rockwell painting of a freckle-faced twelve year old with his hand on the shoulder of a six year old wearing a sweatshirt too big for him, dungarees cuffed four inches above shoes that were untied, a ball cap that still had a toddler-esque logo of a baseball diamond, and you have the proper visage of Tom and me that day.

Tom was a master of motivation. His choice of words, "I need you to do something for me," could not have been more brilliant. He had my rapt attention and full commitment to whatever he was about to request.

"See that fire hydrant *way* down there on the left?"

I followed his gaze and pointed finger.

"Yeah?"

"That's the end zone marker for that end of the field; but see how there's only one?"

At this point I'm feeling so "included," so much a "part" of the hierarchy of the neighborhood. I had arrived. I nodded my head to signal my understanding.

"Here's what I want you to do for me. You go down and be the fire hydrant on the right side of the end zone. That way we'll have markers on both sides."

And I ran happily off to fill my role.

I was the "end zone marker." Important stuff. I vividly

remember standing there on fall Saturdays, the smell of grass and mud, the autumn leaves dancing all around—and me diligently, studiously lining up with the fire hydrant to mark the end zone line. It was a job filled with subtleties— like knowing when to adjust your position on the goal line depends on whether or not your team was defending the goal or trying to score.

And just in case the significance of my role had been lost on me, Tom recapped my contribution on the way home.

"Did you have fun today, Danny?"

"Well . . . I kinda just stood there and watched."

"*Stood there and watched?*" Tom repeated with mock astonishment. "Are you kidding me? Weren't you the guy who signaled touchdown when Kevin snagged that catch in the corner of the end zone?"

"Yeah . . ."

"And didn't we count on your spot when David fumbled on the goal line?"

"Well yeah . . ."

"There you have it. *Without you* we'd of lost by two touchdowns!"

And that's the way I responded to my dad's inquiry as we sat around the family table that night.

"Without me, Dad, we'd of lost by two touchdowns!"

My dad nodded his head in somewhat surprised satisfaction, smacked Tom on the shoulder. Tom winked at me and Kevin—Kevin just kept eating his hot dogs and beans to keep from laughing, no doubt.

Still, I went to bed that night flush with contentment for having earned the adulation of my older brothers. I was not "Danny the Human Fire Hydrant" as I drifted off to sleep that night. Nay, I was "Dangerous Dan Porter: End Zone Monitor, the Arbitrator of Football Fate."

It was my initiation into the neighborhood caste system. You knew your role and you played it for the sake of the game.

You knew if all the older kids were around, you'd have no chance at playing. You also knew that, depending upon your age among the taxi squad members, you might be an end zone marker (*"See the fire hydrant; be the fire hydrant, Danny"*) or you might be all-time snapper (Joey Diamond had the role in front of me, and man did I want it badly because the whole game turned on you for the briefest of moments), all-time line of scrimmage marker—or, on those rare days (as you got older) all-time quarterback. The secret was knowing your role—and looking for the opportunity to advance it.

The skills we first developed playing in neighborhood games carried into our teen years when neighborhood games gave way to organized sports. I remember going up to our high school's varsity coach one night at open gym in the spring. I had played in junior high, missed the cut my freshman year, but stayed around as manager because the coach let me practice with the team. So now I was approaching the summer between my freshman and sophomore year with a staunch determination to make the team. I played ball four to six hours a day on the neighborhood courts, and when I wasn't playing, I was doing drills.

I ran.

I jumped rope.

I weight lifted.

And I waited.

I waited until I turned in a peak performance during a particularly intense pickup game, wherein I recorded a triple double. Triple doubles are like the holy grail of basketball statistics and refer to double-digit performance in any key area of measurable performance: usually in points, rebounds, steals, assists, or blocked shots. For me, I measured triple doubles a bit differently: passes I *actually* caught, passes I threw that *weren't* stolen, and shots taken that were *not* blocked. Having recorded such a feat on this particular evening, I approached the coach.

I had been taught by my older brothers to condition coaches with your hustle and refs with your manners. To condition a coach or ref was to show them your value through the consistency of your behavior. You never "talked a good game"; you "played a good game." If you weren't the best on the floor, make sure they understood no one tried harder than you. That meant diving for every loose ball, admitting every mistake the ref called you for . . . and so forth. I noticed the coach noticing me, and so I went for it.

Our high school varsity coach was so intense that it was not uncommon for tears to form in his eyes. Not weepy tears, tears of frustration as he strained to restrain the urge to throw a chair, or a player in the chair. And though many of his techniques would probably be considered misdemeanors today, none of us mistook his intent. He wanted the best out of you for the best in you. We had the privilege of his tutelage in his high school coaching career. He went on to coach several Division I-A schools at the collegiate level.

"Coach, I'm really working to make the team. I'm playing a lot, working on drills, lifting, running, jumping rope . . . can you see anything else I should be doing?"

He looked right at me and rattled off a list so fast that I was pleased to realize he actually had been thinking about me. At the very least he had noticed me.

"Well, you need to be more willing to take a charge; you need to drive the lane more, keep diving for loose balls, and work on making your defense more annoying to the guy you're covering."

I was pumped. Here he was, the icon of hoops at our high, giving me the recipe to make the team. In my hysteria I moved in for one last affirmation.

"So if I pick it up in those areas, I have a good shot at making the team?"

He turned to me with a surprised look on his face, as if to ask, "Are we having the *same* conversation?" and dished off a statement that still rings in my ears. "Oh hell no . . ." he said to make sure he left no self-delusion in my psyche. "You got exactly no shot at making this team. Your role is to embarrass these stiffs enough that they get off their duffs and work a little harder. After all, if they see *you* doing it, they'll know they had better do it too!"

That was my role. That was my contribution.

Know what I said to him?

"Thanks, Coach. You can count on me."

I had learned to be a "role player" before modern lexicon invented the term. Those lessons of learning to play a lesser role so the greater game could go on took hold; I don't recall ever feeling demeaned by my role. Fortunately for all the neighborhood games we played, the concept of the "inner child" had not yet been discovered, so no one had to worry about long-range damaging effects on me or Joey Diamond for our "all-time" roles.

In fact, I parlayed all those experiences of sighting the end zone line into a summer internship with the county surveyor. It was fine; it all worked out. After playing all-time snapper, young Joey Diamond went to med school, and now he's a proctologist—so it's all good.

Sand Scripts

Your perception
of your role
determines your participation
within it.
Your participation
within your role
determines the perception
 . . . of you.

Occasionally, You Gotta Serve Up a Tater

The importance of mentoring

We called them "taters"; although, I must confess, I'm not altogether sure I know why we did. In the sports speak we emulated at every chance in neighborhood games, a "tater" was a pitch delivered to a batter at precisely that batter's "sweet spot," at precisely the right speed, resulting in said player "mashing" the ball for a long hit, usually a home run. I'm not certain if the reference to the ball as a "tater" had more to do with it appearing soft, round, and full before the batter's view, the resulting "mashing" of the ball, or its location in the "sweet" spot—as in sweet potato pie.

On the notion of what is involved in "serving up a tater," I am infinitely more clear, the meaning of which having been indelibly etched into my memory on Memorial Day of 1972.

Serving up a tater referred to the practice of building confidence in a younger, or less-skilled player, by providing him that choicest of pitches to hit. It had to be done in a way that was not blatantly obvious, or we risked the opposite result of our intention. Lob a pitch in there the wrong way, and everyone knew, including the batter, that you were patronizing his inability.

The undisputed king of tater pitching was my second oldest brother, Kevin. Once I came to know what he was doing, I would stand in my position of left out (fielder) and marvel at his sleight of hand, his skilled deception of making the batter believe he had out-dueled Kevin to get a hit. Kevin would start out smoking two strikes by the batter before yielding the pitch he intended the batter to smash. The signature move that signaled the tater was coming would be a wink Kevin threw to the outfield before turning to face a batter. It was yet another form of contribution in neighborhood games—you took occasion to build another's self-esteem by ensuring their athletic success. I was always in favor of it, having benefited from it myself on many occasions. But this day—this day Kevin's timing and magnanimity could not have come at a less auspicious time.

In the neighborhood I was best friends with Richie Paressi. Richie was eighteen months older than me and two grade levels ahead in school. In such cases the younger neighborhood resident never acknowledged the older when the two met anywhere other than the neighborhood, and certainly you never spoke of the games you played together. However, in the neighborhood, Richie and I did everything together. Played ball, watched TV, went to the drug store, scrounged pop bottles, and traded baseball cards. Richie was a near-permanent resident of our house—owed more to my sibling circle than to me, but I basked in the friendship nonetheless. With two older brothers, who were among the most recognizable athletes in the city, and older sisters Richie swooned around, no one would have questioned why he hung around a fourth grader.

So, when on the Memorial Day Weekend of 1972, Richie had Brad Hatch spending the weekend at his house, they spent most of it at our house. Brad was definitely the Big Man on Campus at our school. Mr. "Everything" athlete, student council president, straight-A student, heart throb, and generally the kind of kid everyone wanted to be like, but no one could. His very presence in our neighborhood, let alone my home, was sure to raise my social stock to an all-time high.

As that Saturday afternoon opened with a game of hoops in our driveway, I remember thinking with reckless abandon that I couldn't wait to get to school that Tuesday.

Okay, so along the course of that weekend I spilled milk on myself, tripped over the hose in the yard, dropped a sure touchdown pass, and sat defenselessly by as my sisters went to great lengths to tell Brad how they used to dress me up as Raggedy Ann on Halloween. I was about to surmount all those setbacks and still arrive at school with a swagger—because here it was, Monday afternoon, all of us assembled on Edison Field for the inaugural summer classic baseball game, the late afternoon sun casting shadows over right and center field . . . and my team ahead of Richie and Brad's by a run in the bottom of the ninth inning.

Every kid who ever picked up a ball glove, however idly or for however long, knows the phrase *"Two men out, two men on, bottom of the ninth, full count."* It describes, in but thirteen syllables, the single most pressurized moment in all of sports. As a batter, you're down to your last pitch—your last chance to do something heroic for your team. If you hit a single, even a blooper, you get carried off the field on the shoulders of your teammates, for your hit had won the game. Equally, for the pitcher and the team on the field, one more strike, one more out, and the celebration began.

At the plate was young Joey Casey. Joey, who was eight and had been included in this game by my next oldest sister, Eileen, hadn't so much as swatted a fly all afternoon. I was feeling good, smacking my hand in my glove and anticipating the sweet ecstasy of besting two upper classman, one a living legend. Brad was on third base, leading off a little and looking back nervously at Richie, who stood a yard or so off second base. I knew what was on their mind as much as they knew what was on mine: they did *not* want to lose this game. The count *was* full; there *were* two outs, two men *were* on, and it *was* the bottom of the ninth.

In my blind bliss I failed to properly assess the moment. Kevin had not.

You see, Joey was the youngest brother in a long line of accomplished Casey family athletes. His older brothers had preceded Kevin through high school, but their legend lived on, and here was Kevin, on the mound, ball in hand, with a chance to show them respect by allowing a member of their proud legacy, a moment of athletic glory.

Kevin turned toward us in the outfield—and winked.

The tater was about to be served.

Something inside of me snapped. I had been well trained to know my place, to know when I could challenge the status quo mandated and maintained by my older brothers and when I could not—as was clearly the case in this moment— but I snapped. If we had been in a movie, you would have seen the cameras drop into super-slow motion as I wildly shook my head, screaming "No! No! No! Time out! Time out!" and running toward the mound.

It was too late. Kevin had already gone through his windup. What happened next passed before me in still-frame progression. Not normally gifted with exceptional athletic vision, I saw the entire sequence with high-definition clarity.

Kevin's arm swung through the throwing motion. I saw the ball release from his grip; I saw Joey's eyes light up at the sight of the pitch hanging in front of him like a piñata begging to be hit; I saw the swing of his bat and the ball careening off his aluminum sword—a certain trajectory toward left field—and I saw myself in baseball's no-man's-land. My momentum ahead of my balance and coordination, I stood helplessly by, watching the seam-over seam rotation of the ball over my outstretched hand as I back peddled into futility and ignominy. Not only did I not catch the ball, I fell on my back-*pride* in the process.

I charged the mound in protest.

"Why'd you let him hit that? You gave away the game! You

gave him a *tater*!"

I was shouting so loudly it momentarily drew attention away from the celebration at home plate, raising the slightest specter of doubt as to the authenticity of young Joey's epic hit. Kevin deftly countered.

"Me? *I* gave away the game? Funny, that didn't look like me sitting on my butt in shallow left while the ball sailed over *my* head."

Richie's team erupted in laughter and returned to their celebration. By now I was close enough to Kevin for him to lower his voice, raise his eyebrows, and issue the edict I never challenged: "Shut your mouth."

On the way home I took up my cause once more.

"I can't believe you served him a tater, right when we were about to win."

"Oh?" Kevin said in a tone that mocked the incredulous position I was taking. "Like we never did that for you? Like we never could have won a game that we let you win instead? Give me a break."

"Yeah, but," I stammered, grasping at straws, "I bet I never cost *you* a game against Paressi and Hatch."

Kevin looked at me in a way that effortlessly expressed he would not be dignifying my quibble with a response. Instead, he said something that has remained with me ever since.

"I'll tell you what, little man, what you *think* you lost, compared to what I *know* he gained . . . is a trade I will make every single time."

Sand Scripts

I have learned
to measure the value of
my contribution
not by what it costs me
to make it,
but by what it means
for those
who receive it.

Of Moon Pies, Mallow Bars, & Mrs. Price

Invaluable lessons in integrity

To this day I can look at neither a Moon Pie, nor a Mallow Bar, and not think of Mrs. Price and her son, Darren "Bubby" Price. In life there are contributions to one's character that can only be delivered by a friend; there are lessons of ethics and emotional maturity you can only learn by making a mistake and being called on it. No parental lecture, no lesson plan, no sermon can embed the value of the lesson in your psyche the way a single look from a friend can. It's the look that tells you you crossed the line; you broke the code; you went too far. I got that look from Bubby Price one day, and I never repeated the course of action that led him to look at me that way.

The Price family had moved to our community from rural Tennessee. Their Southern ways were, at times, a source of amusement to we sophisticated folk from the industrial Northeast. Mr. Price was an over-the-road truck driver who wasn't home all that often and whose stern disposition scared us a bit whenever he was. He believed in short hair which he Brylcreemed to stand on end—at a time when we were all trying to look as mop haired as the Beatles. He wore denim jeans that were as straight legged as he was—at a time when we judged pant coolness by the size of the bell in your bell-bottomed jeans. He listened to country music at a time when, well—you just didn't listen to country music and admit to others that you did.

Bubby wore, listened to, and otherwise preferred everything his father's favor fell upon—an endearing quality, to be sure, but one that put him decidedly out of step with the cool strut of the day. It meant playing with Bubby presented a social risk for a budding sandlotter such as me, a risk that had to be carefully mitigated at every turn. As much as I'd like to claim a higher reason for what motivated me to bridge the chasm between my world of the late 1960s and Bubby's stylings from the mid-1950s, it really came down to Mrs. Price and those mid-afternoon treats.

Mrs. Price always wore a dress, her hair always looked beauty-parlor fresh, and her omnipresent smile was always followed by words like, "honeybunch," "sugar," and "my, oh my." Her sunny disposition, the sort that would make Donna Reed feel inadequate, always seemed to shine brightest when we arrived on her doorstep to call Bubby out to play. Of all their Southern ways, the twang in their voice, the slow drawl of their speech, their incessant politeness to everyone (including each other), and the fact that they named a child "Bubby"— the one quality of the Price family that never drew a snicker from us was their Southern hospitality. Whenever I played at the Price home, I knew at some point Mrs. Price was going to utter that magical phrase: "Can I interest you fine young gentlemen in a little afternoon snack?"

Little afternoon snacks at the Price home nearly outshone birthday celebrations at our house. For us, a family of eight children, a treat was unheard of by and large, and when they did come along, the most you could usually hope for were two sandwich cookies from the local A&P. For Bubby Price, afternoon treats were a staple of his existence, and in this single aspect alone, I envied him greatly.

Mrs. Price would set out glasses of cold milk, followed by the distribution of napkins, and then she would lay out these plates full of high-octane sugar snacks. The treats du jour would vary from Twinkies, cupcakes, Ding Dongs, or Ho Hos, to mallow bars and my personal favorite: moon pies. I remember sitting in that kitchen, the chrome-legged chairs with the vinyl seat cushions that stuck to the sweat on your legs, and salivating as Mrs. Price would pour our milk and assemble the snack tray of the day. I'm not proud that my predilection for pastries fueled my friendship with Bubby, but in truth, it was the driver of my journeys down the block to tap on their door.

The friendship was facilitated by a few key factors that allowed me to pull it off without risking my social status. Bubby occupied a niche in our neighborhood. I was nine at the time, my younger brother Tim was five, and Bubby was six. Technically, he was more Tim's friend than mine, and I could pass off the playtime at the Price plantation as my having to "watch Tim." I was also aided in this double life by the nifty notion that Bubby was never allowed to leave his yard. By never I don't mean "usually" or "on certain occasions"—I mean *never*. With this father on the road so much, I guess Mrs. Price kept her children safe by keeping them at home.

I kept this dance going for two years—sneaking down to play with Bubby when my other neighborhood friends were occupied or simply not home. The games in our neighborhood did not unfold endlessly; there were certain cycles and rhythms to them, and one knew the windows of time wherein your activity could go by unnoticed. It was in these windows of opportunity that I would find a reason to join Tim and Bubby in their afternoon play, and partake of Mrs. Price's treats. I remember how her pleasantness helped ease my guilt; I rationalized that I couldn't be in the wrong when it seemed to bring her so much joy to offer us Moon Pies at midday.

Then came that fateful afternoon when I, in a moment of peer panic, breeched all sense of decorum and good taste and blatantly took advantage of Mrs. Price's generosity.

I was hanging out in our front yard minding my own

business in one of those summer day lulls when nothing seemed enticing enough to engage my attention. I was idling away the hours trying to figure out why the hub caps on car wheels appear to turn the opposite way of the wheels as cars turned the corner at the end of our block when two of my friends from school came riding toward me on their new Stingray bikes, the kind with banana seats and tall "sissy bars," a feature that, in contrast to its name, was the coolest thing a kid could want on his bike.

Their presence on my street represented an immediate social challenge. When friends from school showed up in your neighborhood, your two worlds were set on a collision course. It was a moment that had to be handled with great deftness. If your home milieu didn't match your "cool at school," you were risking the loss of your status there and facing banishment to the fringes of the playground. I was keenly aware of this as Mike Stack and Bobby Reiz were now showing me their new bikes and bragging of their boundary-less romp through our hometown. I was trying to escape the episode without having to show them my bike when Bobby piped up and issued a daunting challenge.

"So Dan, can you give us something to eat? We've been riding all afternoon. How about a pop and something to munch on?"

Two things I knew immediately: the only *pop* we ever had in our house was my dad, and the likelihood of me scoring a socially acceptable snack for them to munch on was as remote as my referring to my father as "Pop."

"Ah, ah," I adroitly articulated the universal syllables of stalling, trying to buy myself some time to think of a way out of the mess I was quickly sinking into, "I could, but I gotta go get my little brother. He's playing at his friend's house and I gotta bring him home now."

A momentary calm settled over my being. I had found a plausible dodge, and to ensure its execution, I turned and headed down the block.

"Hey, we'll come with you," Mike blurted out. "And then you can get something for us when we get back."

I should have stopped right there. I should have simply told my schoolmates that our family didn't dole out sugar snacks on a whim, that my bike was an English racer hand-me-down I hadn't yet learned to master, and that they should enjoy their new wheels and motor along on their way. Instead, I let them follow me, knowing by the set of the sun in the afternoon sky that it was almost treat time at the Price house. Maybe, just maybe, if I feigned an intent to proudly introduce Bubby to my school chums, Mrs. Price would extend them an invitation to munch on mallow bars and moon pies. It was a despicable ploy—and one now set irrevocably in motion.

Seen from a distance, it would have appeared my friends on bikes were escorting me to detention, my aunt's house on a Sunday afternoon, or some other detestable fate. My shoulders were slumped, my stomach was churning, and my mouth was pasty dry. I was anticipating their reaction to Bubby who, likeable as he was one-on-one, was such an anomaly to our sense of cool that to be seen as his friend was to risk everything. Arriving at the front walk of the Price home, my guys dismounted and followed me to the door.

Mrs. Price answered with her signature animated greeting, "Hello, young Danny. Have you come to join the boys to play?"

Join the boys to play. Strike one for me. Before I could respond, Mrs. Price noted the presence of my schoolmates.

"And look, you've brought your other friends along, too. How nice. I don't believe I know these fine young men."

Following my introductions, Mrs. Price turned her attention into her home and threw me a slider so smooth I couldn't even foul it off. "Bubby, Danny has come calling, and he's brought two new friends. Come meet the boys."

Danny has come calling. Social strike number two.

I heard the snickers of my mates at the mere mention of the name *Bubby*, and Mike Stack's arched eyebrows called me on the obvious: I routinely came to the Price home to play.

Tim appeared at the door first, followed by Bubby who, upon seeing the Stingrays, burst through the door and down the walk, saying something like, "Dang, look at these b-eye-kes."

His twang lilting on the single syllable of the word "bike," his vernacular as anachronistic as his plaid shirt with tin buttons, Bubby now physically stood on the walkway between me and my school friends.

"Hey, you guys wanna play?" he asked with complete disregard for the notion that he was entering fourth grade, and we, sixth. He was foolhardy enough to believe other kids my age indulged in play beneath their age level—and he was genuine enough that he never suspected my trips to his yard were less so. In his zeal and excitement, he reared back and smoked a fastball down the middle of the plate so fast I never even got the bat off my shoulder.

"Danny, I broke your Monkey Ball record! I tossed thirty-six of them in the trash can—din't miss a one. . . ."

I felt all the blood drain from my head, my torso, my arms, and my legs and pool in my feet, making them feel like lead. In a span of time no longer than a lightning flash, I knew I was never going to get the chance to explain that "Monkey Balls" were not an anatomical feature of animals, but a name given to the nuts that fell from the trees in the Price yard. I instinctively and instantly knew I would no longer be referred to as "Dan the Man" at school, a very cool moniker my third grade gym teacher had given me, and one I had cultivated into my personal branding campaign. No, from this point forward I knew Mike and Bobby would ensure I'd forevermore be known as "Danny the Monkey Ball Boy."

Mrs. Price's angelic voice pierced my sudden darkness. "Danny, the boys were just about to have snack. Would you and your friends care to join them?"

A momentary respite, a chance of redemption, and a plausible explanation I could circle back to—I didn't come down here to *play*; it was all about the treats.

Our faces, half-a-moon deep into the chocolate-covered graham crackers with marshmallow filling, a telling moment came upon me. Mrs. Price had gone into the laundry room, Bubby had gone to his room to retrieve something, and Tim was eating the last of his treat. If I didn't act quickly, there was going to be an expectation that me and my boys had actually come to play.

"C'mon Tim, we gotta go home now. . . ." I said to Tim, hoping the sternness of my tone would deflect any objections he would have to the contrary.

"No we don't. It's not time for dinner. Aren't you going to stay and play?"

"We *gotta* go. *Mom* said."

"No we don't. Mom's not even home today—and you know it."

Somewhere along the way I had failed to teach my younger brother to recognize the language of deception and respond in kind. Now I stood alone, out on a limb. Mike Stack happily shook that limb.

"So *Danny*, you come to play here a lot?" He asked in a thick mocking whisper.

"Yeah," Bobby chimed in, "is *Bubby* your best friend?"

To this day I cringe at what happened next. Backed into a corner by my own hand, I played the only card I had left; and, sadly, it was the truth.

"No way! Are you kidding? I only come down here for these!"

I thrust my finger in the direction of the moon pies that filled our plates. I turned to see if Mrs. Price could have possibly heard my confession and, instead, I found myself looking into Bubby's blank expression. He had returned in time to hear my despicable declaration. The look on his face, the blank stare of a hero into the eyes of his betrayer, was more than I could bear and I remember it to this day.

Mrs. Price, humming gently, returned to the room and now stood behind Bubby. "Just leave those dishes right there boys. I'm sure you're anxious to play."

Bubby never turned his head, never took his gaze off me. Here, this nine-year-old son of the South, naïve and guileless, had the presence of mind to understand his mother's generosity was being taken advantage of and he would have none of it.

"No ma'am," he said, his voice suddenly twang-less and lilt-less. "Dan and his friends were just leaving."

"Oh . . ." Mrs. Price said in slow surprise. Picking up on the tension in the room, she politely expressed pleasure for meeting my friends, and before I knew it, I was walking back up the slate walkway to my home.

I don't remember much of what happened next. I suppose my friends went on their way and forgot about the exchange. The consequences of which I had been so afraid were forgotten by the time they parked their bikes back at their homes.

Tim continued to play at the Price house for the two years we remained in that neighborhood. However, I never returned to while away the hours in such idle delights of tossing fallen fruit into empty trashcans, hearing the thud of success striking the galvanized tin. I never again experienced the unbridled excitement of Bubby calling out to me as I turned up his sidewalk. I never again could look at a Moon Pie and not have the taste of compromised integrity in my mouth. It was a hard lesson to have learned, but learn it I did. I never again abused the kindness of a friend, the hospitality of their families, nor the generosities lavished on me.

Sand Script

I am grateful
to those of my friends
who always accepted me
as I am.
I am indebted
to those of my friends
who expected me to be
all I am capable
of being.

Improvise

Lines Are Words in a Play

Two Will Get You Twenty

The Gordon Bradshaw Rule

Improvise

*Do what you can
with what you have
where you are.*
—*Theodore Roosevelt*

I'm going to hazard a guess that not many of my neighborhood comrades in arms could have told you who Teddy Roosevelt was, but we all lived by this creed of the original *Rough Rider*.

Discretionary spending had not yet found its way to the underage group of our day. There weren't mega-sports stores in every plaza. A new baseball bat came around about as often as the Olympics. So when the bladder of your football was coming through the laces, when your basketball held air only as long as a twenty-four-second clock, you pioneered new uses for shoe laces, your mom's old nylons, and duct tape—so you could play.

A stone and three sections of sidewalk kept us hopscotching our way through an idle afternoon. Any eight-foot band of cotton fibers became our jump rope and provided an afternoon of aerobic exercise that, if you had told us it was such, we would have avoided. An empty can, rocks to throw, or nothing but the will to run with reckless abandon were all we needed for a game to begin. As much as we improvised materials, it was also our ability to choreograph play in the limits of physical space that gave shape and dimension to our games.

While it is true that necessity is the mother of invention, it was scarcity that acted as the incubator for the development of our ability to adapt, to adjust, and to create facsimiles reasonable enough to suspend doubt and allow our play to continue.

Consider "ghost men," if you will. Ghost men were the single greatest invention of our time. Two kids could play a nine-inning game of baseball because their "dugouts" were filled with a wide array of imaginary players we could call upon in a moment's notice. We could count on ghost men in a way we could count on no other. They never ran on a long fly ball with only one out. They never got thrown out because they dogged it down the base paths. They never got picked off taking too big a lead, nor did they ever get caught in a pickle. They were the essence of dependability in our neighborhood game world.

We named our ghost men and called on them in accordance with the needs of the day. We had Ruth, Clemente, Gehrig, DiMaggio, and Brock . . . all the great ones played in our neighborhood. It added to the drama because while we had ghost men as our alter egos, one of us inevitably had to play the role of hall of fame play-by-play man, Phil Rizzuto.

"Tight situation here at Fenway. Two out, two men on, bottom of the ninth. Lou Brock is on third; Davey Lopez on second as Niekro looks in for the sign . . ."

It was all strategy and drama . . . and it happened every day. Today they call it "Fantasy Baseball Camp" and you pay ten thousand dollars for the experience.

Ghost men helped you learn important strategies of baseball, like advancing the runner. If you blooped a single to left, you called out, "Ghost man on first!" You had to call it out. If you didn't, it didn't count, and you lost that runner. You had to always notify your opponent as to the presence of your poltergeist players because while ghost men could score for you, they could also accumulate your outs.

You smacked one over the pitcher's head and made it to

first before the ball got back to the pitcher. "Ghost man on first and second!"

We learned to balance out advantages and minimize disadvantages—like the rule about throwing the ball back to the pitcher. No one could possibly cover all the infield positions and make plays at first from the pitcher's mound. So, the provision became the toss back to the pitcher. If the pitcher had the ball in his mitt before your foot hit the bag, you were out. Not that that was ever cause for an argument.

If you had ghost men on first and second, and you happened to hit a sharp grounder down the third baseline, a capable in/out fielder could scoop up your grounder, tag third, and make the short throw to the pitcher and double you up in no time flat.

Challenges led to innovations.

Obstacles were obliterated by imaginative solutions.

"Imagination is more important than knowledge," Einstein once said, "[because] knowledge is limited."

Einstein . . . now there's a ghost man you'd definitely want as your manager.

Faced with the limitations of time and space, our days playing neighborhood games exacted from us the ability to *improvise.*

Lines Are Words in a Play

Refuse to accept the limitations of convention

"Where are the baselines?"

My friend from a crosstown gated community on the edge of the golf course with every amenity imaginable asked as he stood in our driveway where we had assembled for the afternoon's baseball game.

"*Lines?* Who needs lines?" I cajoled.

"Lines!" Richie Paressi chimed in like a Vaudeville comedian picking up on his feeder line. "Ain't those the things an actor says in plays?"

A self-satisfied laugh later, I outlined our beloved sandlot baseball field.

"Stop sign is first base. The big rock at the end of that third driveway—that's second base. Street sign is third. We bat from the bottom of our driveway."

With the infield outlined, Richie continued with the outfield.

"Yearnst Street is out of bounds for right field; Lawson Street is out of bounds for left field. If you hit Franzinger's lawn on the fly—automatic home run. If you hit the fence in Selnick's yard—that's a ground-rule double. If you hit Kuehn's yard—automatic out."

Our ball fields did not have meticulously edged white lines or groomed surfaces. There were no "grids" in our gridirons; our baseball fields never conjured an image of anything as geometrically exquisite as a "diamond"—and the only thing resembling a court for our basketball games were the arguments. In fact, many a sandlotter became a deft dribbler, gold-glove shortstop, or tight-rope-walking receiver by learning to navigate the rocks, potholes, and narrow confines of our fields of play.

Gather a gang of retired neighborhood gamers, take them back to the fields of their youth, and almost without exception the first comment you'll hear is, "How did we ever manage to play here?" Innovation. Plain and simple. Good old-fashioned youthfully exuberant innovation. And when even our imaginative eyes found limitations to the physical space available from which to craft a field, we turned our attention to the remaining great determining factor of our foibles: the rules.

For example, we could play an enormously challenging, engaging, exhausting game of football on a street as tight as 146th Street in Queens, New York—cars parked on both sides of the street—by adjusting the rules.

"Tom bats lefty."

"Kevin gets two strikes only."

"Three outs for us; two outs for you, 'cause we got Danny on our side."

We shaped, sketched, and innovated play in a way the most talented video game designers still cannot.

"Street light to street light are the end zones," someone would call out as a ceremonial means of establishing the rules of the contest.

"Three completes is a first down. Only one first down per possession. Five Mississippi rush, one mad-dog rush per four downs."

And then we played.

We ran a lot of hitch-n-go patterns, used the shovel pass, and occasionally the flea-flicker . . . and we played.

Watching a top-flight NFL quarterback throw a fade to the corner of the end zone to a spot only his receiver could reach, while facing the certainty of being hit by an oncoming defensive lineman, is indeed a thing of beauty. It pales in comparison, though, to watching my brother, Kevin, loft a spiral to me, inches away from the stop sign at the corner of 159th and East–North Broadway—just as the rapid-transit bus was approaching its stop—and I've got the grille marks to prove it.

I was recently speaking on innovation at a business conference, using this example of our creativity in forming fields of play and games of chance from the confines of our neighborhoods, when an elderly Italian gentleman approached me on a break.

"Ah," he began with a nostalgic, melancholic sigh, "from the sounds of the ball fields you played on growing up, I can tell you come from a privileged background."

Always game for this generational battle of comparisons, I laughed and said, "Privileged compared to what?"

"Hey," he replied, in a New York City accent as thick as his hands, mustache, and ruddy torso, "as kids we played stickball in the alleyway behind Kennicky's bakery!"

"You played baseball . . . in an alleyway?"

"Sure. We all did." Sensing a rapt audience, he waxed both nostalgic and poetic, one hand in his suit pants pocket, the other painting his words on the air. "You placed your catcher by the street and you played *into* the alley, see. We took a piece of chalk and had marks on the wall, at different heights, see— one for a single, another meant a double, then the triple and the only automatic home run was straight back and high up on the back wall of the alley—which could be a hundred feet or so away. You hit a window—you were out, or if someone caught it or you struck out.

"We'd play for hours in that alleyway, the smell of old man Kennicky's bakery just making your mouth water. One of us always tried to sneak in and score a roll or two, and he'd chase us out. The truth is, I think he left a dozen or so there for us most of the time.

    "The smells.

    "The sounds.

    "Yeah, we played some classic games there."

    Where we played greatly impacted how we played. One's zeal to make a catch is intensified when an alleyway wall or oncoming bus is your boundary marker. Our limitations served to sharpen our focus and had us playing eternally in the present moment.

Sand Scripts

Of all the riches
my youth lavished upon me
perhaps the greatest
was the need
to rise above
the perceived limitations
of my circumstances.

Two Will Get You Twenty

How to provide incentives for the overwhelmed and under-qualified

Trashcans don't move.

They are completely predictable.

While they offer a symbolic obstacle that must be momentarily overcome, they have no element of animated chaos, no X-factor, and no random movement that precipitated deft athletic adjustment.

That's where I came in.

My older brother, Kevin, in his endless quest to hone his burgeoning basketball skills, was always rigging up a piece of exercise equipment, an obstacle course, or a challenge-cup match with we, the under-accomplished, if not unable, of the neighborhood. Getting others to play when they are clearly over-matched was a requisite skill for the more athletically accomplished among us.

His dedication was legendary. In the pre-entitlement era we grew up in, the notion of exercise equipment for yourself, let alone your children, was as foreign as a rotary phone is today. As kids we improvised our workouts, both in equipment and in drills to build skill.

I remember watching Kevin do bicep curls with cinder blocks. I remember him throwing fifty pound bags of water softener salt over each shoulder so he could do calf raises with some notion of resistance. I remember him running sprints in the front yard, carrying buckets filled with water as he ran. All these measures sufficed to enhance his physical conditioning—and believe me when I tell you that he was in *great* condition.

Building his basketball skills in the idle hours, the in-between times when there wasn't enough time to get to the high school court or muster up a good pick-up game, was a bit more challenging. I remember him placing trashcans around our court so he could practice spin moves around them. He used to place step ladders with lawn rakes affixed to them to practice getting the right arch on his shots. He even used lawn furniture, precariously placed under the basket, as a means of enticing him to jump higher for rebounds.

When he tired of those drills, he would entice one of us into a game of one-on-one.

As automatic and endless as I may have conveyed our neighborhood games to be, there were times when one, some, or all of us, just didn't feel like playing. It was a particular risk to the over-accomplished. Let's face it, kids are kids, and we mostly did want to play all the time—but the prospect of standing around with your jaw gaping wide open while someone else waltzed, danced, pirouetted, and otherwise trounced you to oblivion in an athletic competition was not something we signed up for daily.

On the one hand, you risked being called out; on the other hand, you risked having your pride rubbed out. Even we learned the concept that there are some risks not worth taking.

"Danny, come play me a little one-on-one," Kevin would call out, dribbling the ball through his legs, off the hood of the car, across the wrought-iron rail of the porch, and then against my head, never missing a bounce nor a beat.

"I don't wanna. . . ."

"Oh, come on. Why not?"

"'Cause all I do is watch you score; then you steal the ball from me; then you score again; then I watch you again; then you score again."

"So, what's the problem?"

"The problem is that's about as much fun as Aunt Ida's on a Sunday afternoon." Aunt Ida's house smelled like a combination of linament and meatloaf and she covered her furniture in plastic.

"Okay, I got a deal for you. . . ."

The key was to entice the lesser player with a scenario tantalizingly close to neighborhood game hall of fame status—the stuff of sandlot immortality. That's what Kevin would do. He'd offer you a contest that allowed him a significant challenge, as in placing himself against seemingly insurmountable odds, and place you within a silent prayer of victory to create a scenario that fully engaged the both of us.

"You listening, Dan-my-man? Here's the game . . . two will get you twenty—and we play to twenty-two."

Looking at him like a puppy dog unsure of his master's command, he elaborated.

"We play the game up to twenty-two points; you have to win by four—you with me so far?"

"Uh-huh."

"The first shot I make is worth two points, like all baskets I make. The first shot you make is worth twenty points—and then you just need to make one more basket after that and you win!"

In the immortal words of my friend, Wendell Adams, "I'm just some dumb, I'm not plumb dumb." I knew it was still highly unlikely I'd win . . . but, boy, a few lucky shots and my big brother was never going to hear the end of it.

"Okay, I'll play!" I said, springing into action, adrenaline pumping, mind racing, and pride salivating.

"Well now, wait a minute. . . ." the con continued. "Since I am really up against it, how about a little wager here . . . a little skin in the game? If I win, you have to stay out here and rebound five hundred foul shots for me. If you win, I'll take you and your fellas to the DQ after dinner."

I contemplated the risk. Rebounding five hundred foul shots could take an hour or more . . . and it made me long for Aunt Ida's. Still . . . DQ with my crew?

"Deal."

"Good man," Kevin confirmed, "and, oh yeah, we're playing 'make-it-take-it.'"

Make-it-take-it meant you kept control of the ball as long as you scored. If you made the basket, you got the ball back.

You can surmise the rest.

Kevin led the league in free throw percentage that season, and I never got so much as a whiff of the Dairy Queen. Oh sure, I got close a few times. Some of the scores of our contests made it all the way up to thirty-eight to thirty-four, and in those moments on the edge, on the cusp of greatness, on the fringe of the immortal, I remember feeling so alive. I'd be racing for a rebound, trying to lob up a shot to win, and Kevin would be reaching for the heights of his athleticism to prevent ignominy.

That's what kids did for each other in our day. We created plausible outcomes from implausible circumstances. We compromised to bridge chasms of capabilities in a way that made great accomplishments just a shot or two away for either one of us.

"Bobby, I bet I can hit the stop sign ten times before you hit it once."

Or *"We'll spot you five and play to ten."*

Other than serving as our introductory course to statistics and probability (there wasn't a mathematician among us, yet all of us could give you odds, tell you your winning percentage, your batting average, and your standard deviation—on the spot), the real gift of our quest to create a match from mismatched skill levels was the practice it gave us in creating win-win scenarios. It was all about the give-and-take.

"You guys play kickball with us today, and we'll play

capture the flag with you tonight."

We may as well have been saying, "If you give me a shot at my dream, I'll give you a shot at yours."

Now those are risks worth taking.

Sand Scripts

If you don't occasionally
give wing
to the silliest notions
of your spirit,
how can you expect
your dreams of fancy
to take flight?

The Gordon Bradshaw Rule

Find a way to play—or make one

There is a sound a basketball makes when it is bounced outside on a cold winter day. The normal baritone bounce sound is replaced with a high-pitched ping, almost a whine. The normal cadence of a deft dribbler on a summer day is replaced with a series of the solitary outbursts of one being spanked as players slammed the ball to the ground in an increasingly futile effort to make it bounce. You just couldn't play basketball on a winter's day when the temperature was in the single digits and the wind chill was taking the ambient air temperature south of the zero mark.

That is, unless you were Gordon Bradshaw.

Gordon Bradshaw would play hoops in any weather, and arctic air never deflated the bounce of his basketball. He would play until his fingers and lips were cracked and bleeding from the cold. He was tan in the winter, a skier's tan, and yet he never set a ski on a slope. He just played and the ball always bounced.

I first met Gordon when my family moved from a suburb of Cleveland, Ohio, to one near Youngstown, Ohio. And though the two communities were separated only by a sixty-seven mile stretch of Interstate 76, they may as well have been on either side of the country. We moved in the middle of my sixth grade year. And for me, given my as yet undiagnosed multifocal dystonia, the transition was anything but welcome.

It impacted all my siblings except for my eldest sister who was, at the time, already in college. The days of our move fell in the middle of December during an unusually cold snap of weather that only added to our feelings of isolation.

We didn't meet anyone in the new neighborhood during that first week of our residence there. We always attended the local Catholic grade school, which meant that unless the kids in your neighborhood went there, as well, you didn't meet them. I remember how creepy it felt in our new house because at night we didn't yet have blinds or curtains on the windows, and as the darkness descended and the lights rose inside the house, you felt like you were inside a fish bowl. We felt like subjects in an experiment, like we were on one side of a two-way mirror and we had no idea who was on the other side.

We had no bearings because kids in our day always defined the quality and comfort of a home by the number of kids around to play with. From inside our box-laden home, we couldn't tell if we had moved into a neighborhood filled with kids or a retirement village.

Then came that sound.

I was in my bedroom stuffing, rather "storing," things in the back of my new closet when I first heard it. It landed with a blare on my consciousness.

As I moved to the window to investigate it further, I heard my older brothers coming down the hallway to the back of the house to investigate the sound, as well. My younger brother and I had the best view in the house—two side-by-side windows framing the urban panoramic vista. The streets that outlined our neighborhood were broken into short blocks, and the lots, equally as shallow as the blocks, were short. All formed a sort of common area in the back of our homes. It was broken only by the occasional tree. So, coming to my second-story bedroom window gave one a bird's eye view of any activity anywhere within that city block. We must have been a sight, four young men standing in descending height and age order, scanning the landscape for the source of the sound. We had all heard what I would describe as a sort of rapid-fire "pinging."

Then he emerged, a graceful figure breaking past the end of his house along the narrow strip of concrete, gliding toward the hoop that hung from the peak of his family's two-car garage. The basketball was obediently bounding back to him in spite of the outside temperature being a balmy twelve degrees (several early morning trips out to the family wagon had prompted a call to the local weather line, and so we were all keenly aware of the frigid day—a background factoid that made our current view all the more remarkable).

You couldn't help but notice a few things about Gordon. He was quick. He darted about the court like an ice cube on a linoleum countertop. He had a great post-up jump shot. And, he could dribble, a reference both to his athletic ability and the bounce-ability of the ball.

I don't recall any of us saying a word to each other. That's another thing we learned in our youth—the art of movement as communication, the unspoken and yet crystal clear dialog among the tribesman of the games.

We split up in order to do what we knew must get done.

You didn't "ask" for permission to go out and play. You executed maneuvers. Dialogue with your parents, in most cases children of the Depression Era for whom work was the backbone of all human value, was a certain invitation to more chores, or lectures. No, we never pitched the plea, "Dad, can I go play with the guys?" We simply fulfilled our responsibilities and reported their completion with military-like efficiency.

"Dad, I cleaned out the garage, restacked the newspapers, emptied all the trashcans, *and* refilled the windshield wiper fluid in Mom's car."

You only reported completed activities or chores, and you did so in a way that conveyed you knew you were only doing what was expected. The key was in the "and." The "and" was that intangible element you added without being asked.

It was huge. It showed responsibility and commitment, the kind of thing that earned you the right to go and "play." If you could make the "and" something that showed consideration for your mother—you were golden.

You gave your report and . . . you waited. If Dad didn't give you more to do, it was understood that you were vacating the premises at that point.

As important as it was to always add some*thing* else to your report of completed chores, it occasionally became necessary to add some*one* else. If you were detecting shifts in the parental tectonic plates, if you smelled that your day of participating in the neighborhood games was at all in doubt, it was perfectly acceptable to toss a sibling under the bus in order to preserve your ability to go out and play.

"Dad, I cleaned out the garage, restacked the newspapers, emptied all the trashcans, and refilled the windshield wiper fluid in mom's car. Oh, and Tom used your power drill outside and it was kinda muddy, so I cleaned it up and put it back away."

At this point, Dad would be grinding his teeth and flashing a tight-lipped sardonic smile and saying, "Why don't you have Thomas come see me. . . ."

"Do you want me to do anything else, Dad?"

"No—you go play. Just send Thomas to see me."

The "game" was bigger than any of us, and we all understood that.

So, the fact that all four of us arrived at the backdoor of our new home within an hour of hearing the pinging was not at all surprising to any of us. We cut through our backyard, instinctively went to the back edge of our neighbor's yard, and walked along the grass behind their garage (there was a code in those days—you never walked in someone else's yard, but, if there was a strip of land behind their garage, it was a easement—heck, it may as well have been a sidewalk) and arrived court side to get a closer view of this Viking-esque hoopster.

"Hey . . ."

Thomas was my eldest brother by six years; Kevin was four years older; and Tim was four years younger. It was Tom who had offered the universal icebreaker among neighborhood kids. Gordon, who appeared to be somewhere between my age and Kevin's, dutifully reciprocated the syllable.

"Hey."

Gordon shot, the ball bounced back to Tom, eighteen feet out on the right baseline, and he promptly drained a jumper—all net. By now I had placed myself in rebounding position beneath the bucket. I scooped up the shot and dished it out to my older brother, Kevin, who performed a spin maneuver around Gordon, switched the ball from his right hand to his left, and, leaping high enough to dunk the ball, finger rolled it into the ice-starched net.

Kevin had, as they say now, *mad game*, and I learned traveling with him was always a guaranteed invitation to play. He had an incredible ability to slice to the basket, a skill we later determined was born of playing two-on-two on a slab of concrete just large enough for my dad to park his Ford LTD.

Gordon was grinning from ear-to-ear, and I slyly avoided demonstrating any athletic ability by always kicking the ball back out up top.

That was it. A few seconds of athletic prowess from my brothers and we were legendary additions to the neighborhood. I kicked another rebound out to my brother, Tom, and, as the ball hit the concrete and came right into his awaiting hands, he made the comment we'd all been waiting to make.

"This ball's got a lot of bounce. What do you have in it . . . helium?"

Gordon smiled with the joy only an innovator could know. "Nah, it's not helium—just air." Gordon disappeared around the side of his house and reappeared holding a second basketball in his hands.

"What I do, see," Gordon said, knowing he had our undivided attention, "is I take one ball and put it under the dryer vent. The exhaust from the dryer expands the air in the ball and lets me play on cold days. It's normally only good for twenty minutes; that's why it's great to have another basketball on hand."

"What do you do on days when your mom's not doing laundry?" I naively asked.

Gordon looked at Tom and Kevin as if to ask if I was kidding, and then retorted, "You can run a dryer any day of the week and I know how to turn one on . . ."

Genius. Pure, unadulterated genius. In spite of the limitations of the environment, in defiance of nature's edicts, his game went on. That's the essence of **The Gordon Bradshaw Rule**: *find a way to play—or make one.*

Sand Scripts

As fortune
favors the prepared,
so, too, does circumstance
smile on those
who have learned
to adapt.

Compromise

Trade for Stale Bubblegum

"I Call," "Do Over," & "Ollie-Ollie-in-Free"

Under the Shade of the Dogwood Tree

Compromise

*It is literally true that you
can succeed best and quickest
by helping others to succeed.*
—Napoleon Hill

As I have toured the country speaking with individuals and audiences about the lost ways of neighborhood games, many of us have come to recognize that perhaps the greatest contribution our hours of neighborhood play gave us was not the development of athletic prowess, but the formation of our interpersonal skills. Tucked inside the endless hours of play, incubated in the safety of the familiar, and germinated by the relevance of the moment, were the seeds of our emotional intelligence.

From our days of peer-to-peer play, we learned invaluable lessons in integrity, adaptability, negotiating, logical consequences, conflict resolution, motivation, and so much more.

We began to see the effects we had on others because feedback from your peers was immediate and unfiltered. The messages returning to us increased our identification with our interpersonal attributes. We developed problem-solving skills, as well, because our neighborhood days were not idyllic endless sitcoms where everything worked out neatly within the thirty minutes they were on the tube.

I began to wonder how to encapsulate all the lessons in

interpersonal skills into a single attribute of neighborhood games whose name would represent the great intrinsic value those experiences gave us. I had originally listed "Negotiate" and briefly considered "Adaptability" and "Integrity" because they also represented parts of what I believed we learned. Yet, none of those labels seemed to solidify the depth and breadth of this invaluable attribute of our life in the neighborhood.

I began to contemplate "Compromise" as a possibility. I reached for my trusty hardback-bound, have had it for thirty years, doesn't contain words recently invented, *Webster's New World Dictionary of the American Language – Collegiate Edition.* I looked up *compromise*, and here's what I discovered:

Compromise: *1. a settlement in which each side gives up some demands or makes concession*

That definition made some sense to me; we did that all the time. We negotiated in order to get games of skill or chance underway. I remember many a compromise my brothers made to allow for an equitable contest.

Tom would say something like, "Okay, I'll take Danny on my team, but you have to give me an extra out, and every run he scores should count double."

Kevin would mull it over a bit . . . then the look of a distant memory recounting the last time I actually scored a run in a game would trigger a sense of awareness or perhaps fair play and he would say, "Okay, but we get last ups."

"Deal."

Compromise: *2. an adjustment of opposing principles, systems, etc., by modifying some aspects of each*

We did this quite a bit, as well. Monopoly comes to mind. Whereas we mostly learned the physical games, we played from "neighborhood group study" —the games of chance were first introduced within our homes, from our families, and extended families. We learned card games and board games when the whole family came over for Thanksgiving and no one was out playing in the neighborhood. Cousin Katie would bust out a deck of cards and teach us all how to play Hearts, or Spades, or Euchre. The real cerebral games like Chess, Stratego, or Risk—they were being played in the parlor by the older cousins.

This family-centric learning model introduced great variability to the same games when we'd convene to play them in the neighborhood. Be it precipitated by rain, heat, or boredom with the usual array of games, we'd sometimes choose to play Monopoly on a mid-summer day, and the start of those games were always an occasion for compromise.

Player 1: "What are you doing with that five hundred dollars?"

Player 2: "I'm putting it in the middle of the board. You get it if you land on

Free Parking."

Player 3: "Yeah, we do that, too; and, we put all the money you pay from

Community Chest or Chance in there too.

Player 2:"Yep, and the property tax square."

Player 1:"That's not in the rules. . . . Show me where that is in the rules."

Player 3:"Oh God, you play by *those* rules?"

Player 1: "Well yeah . . . except the rule about not being able to put up houses

until all the properties are sold . . . that's a stupid rule; we play that

you can put up houses as soon as you own all the properties in that

set."

Player 2: "Okay, we'll play that way—if we can leave the

money in for Free
   Parking."
   Player 1: "Deal."
   Player 3: "Oh, and if you own the railroads, you can't own
Park Place and
   Boardwalk, too. . . ."

Compromise: *a) exposure, as of one reputation, to danger, suspicion, or disrepute; b) a weakening, as of one's principles*

It's an interesting word, *compromise*. When you delve into its meaning, you find the spectrum of interpersonal life lessons we learned from neighborhood play. The first definitions represent the artful lessons of adaptability and negotiating; the latter represents how we learned the value of integrity by being exposed to the logical consequences of compromising our principles. The last thing we wanted in our neighborhood life was to be known as a cheater, a welcher, a person who couldn't be trusted. There was something powerful about peer-to-peer expectations that largely kept us focused on the higher definitions and purposes of interpersonal skills.

It was the last thing I noticed about the definition of *compromise* that solidified it as the choice for naming this attribute. It was tucked in the etymological references I occasionally glance at in dictionaries. When you translate the word from its roots, it means literally: *together to promise.*

   That's what we did.

Together we promised to give-and-take in our effort to create win-win situations before we knew to call them such.

Together we promised to try to include everyone to a level that made it interesting for them while preserving the competitive spirit of the contests.

Together we promised to abide by the terms and conditions we set forth.

Together we lived with consequences of the promises we

broke . . . and in that learning we grew.

Here then, is the fourth lesson I learned from neighborhood games: Compromise. In my *Streetlights*-rendition of the definition, it means *"to learn the art of growing together **with** promise."*

For it was our ability to compromise that kept us playing together, and when we played together, *anything* was possible.

Trade for Stale Bubblegum

Learning to value experiences over possessions

In our neighborhood the uncontested king of negotiation was a guy by the name of "Johnny O." He was brutal to deal with in negotiations because he always bargained from a position of strength. I don't recall a single situation in which he got less than he wanted. The best times in our neighborhood turned on his benevolence and/or our willingness to cave into his demands. Today he's either an agent or a high-priced defense attorney; of this I am sure.

Here's the thing—everything was better when Johnny played. He knew it and we knew it. The equipment, playing conditions, snacks, and quality of play were unparalleled. He was one of those rare guys who made everyone play better when he played. Somewhere in the process we learned, the rest of us, to become bit players because we couldn't compete for the limelight with Johnny around.

Sensing this, we all, in unspoken agreement, decided the way to manage Johnny was to poor-mouth everything about our existence and maximize his drive to be the superior one who, occasionally and magnanimously, consented to play with us.

It was a conspiracy of commoners against the king, and it worked well. That is, until Easter one year when my visiting uncle gifted me with five dollars. That five-dollar gift nearly disrupted the balance of our neighborhood play for the rest of that spring, summer, and fall.

All of us who had bounded together in the second-tier existence of neighborhood play in that tiny hamlet corner of McLaughlin and North Broadway were coming into our own, from a standpoint of coordination and physical ability. It was promising to be the best stretch of neighborhood games we had ever enjoyed.

Until my Uncle Jim laid that Lincoln in my lap.

I took that five-dollar gift to the local drug store and bought an entire *box* of Topps baseball cards. It was a reckless act, but—hey—I had access to cash and it was Opening Day weekend. I remember walking back from the store, opening pack after pack of cards. The baseball gods had been kind— this box was loaded with the top stars of the day.

Johnny was at the end of his driveway as I walked passed. In my excitement, I showed him my bounty, and he helped me separate the cards into their appropriate hierarchy and also helped himself to most of the stale bubble gum in the box.

The next day we all arrived at Johnny's front door. He had the bat, he had the ball, and his yard was most of our infield and a significant portion of left field.

"Ready to play, Johnny?"

In what followed, he was masterful. I remember his methods to this day.

"Sure. Did you guys bring a bat?"

"No."

"Okay, we'll use mine. Did you bring a ball?"

"No."

"Okay, we'll use mine."

Johnny's grasp of the obvious was becoming somewhat annoying. He knew why we had come, what we wanted, and what we needed. "Where do you want to play?"

"Well," I stammered because his mother was within earshot in their kitchen. "Like we always do, you know . . . here."

"Great!" he responded with enthusiasm. Turning over his shoulder, he delivered the clincher. "Mom, can I take this box of Twinkies out for the guys?"

"Sure," she responded with angelic glee. Secretly, we all hated Johnny. Well, at the least, we deeply envied him.

So we stepped out of his garage onto the blacktop as he went to fetch his Louisville Slugger. Moments later Johnny reappeared, with gear, with goodies, and with an agenda.

"Oh, hey . . . before we get started today, I wanted to trade baseball cards with you, Dan; you got some really good ones yesterday."

Looking more for the Twinkies to be thrown my way and not the angle being played, I replied, "Sure, I got lots of doubles. Which ones do you want?"

"Your Steve Carlton, Gaylord Perry, and Dick Allen—I need those cards."

I laughed aloud. I am sure he did. Carlton and Perry were Cy Young winners, and all Allen did was earn MVP honors the year before.

"Yeah, right, and what are you going to give me?"

"Well, I don't have many doubles right now."

Johnny was creating tension in the crew of players around me and I could feel their impatience rising.

"So what are *you* going to give *me*?" I repeated.

"All the gum from the cards I have gotten or will get this year."

"*What?* Are you crazy? What do I need with stale bubble gum?"

"Hey, don't get mad at me—there's nothing wrong with asking for a trade; they're just some baseball cards."

Now my fellas turned on me. "Yeah, what's the big deal? You got a whole box . . . just give him what he wants and let's play."

I dug in. This was extortion, and since I had, at the time, no idea what extortion meant, I was doubly angry.

95

"No way. I'm not trading."

There was a chill in the warm spring air. Johnny played his part to the hilt. Acting wounded, and moving slowly, he spoke as one dying.

"Look . . . hey, it's okay. I just thought you might want to do something for me 'cause I try to do what I can for you guys. It's not easy asking my mom for those Twinkies, you know. But hey, it's okay. Tell you what, though, I'm feeling kinda bad about all this. I don't think I feel like playing any more today."

Where was the reasonability? Where were my guys coming to my defense to say how enormously crazy this proposed trade was? Silence. Angry silence. There would be no game today.

It went on for a week or better. Since all the guys in the neighborhood went to public school and I to the local parochial, the chasm only widened. I wasn't caving in this time, and Johnny wasn't relenting. Without the two of us, a ball, a bat, or a field, no one played. A fact that kept pressure on the situation.

The following weekend was all I could stand. All the other kids in the neighborhood were high schoolers who had mostly moved on past neighborhood ball. If I didn't put our squad of junior high players back together and back on the field, there'd be nothing else to do.

I remember holding my baseball card trifecta in my hands as I sat on the floor of my bedroom. Maybe I'd get lucky again later that summer, I rationalized. Maybe the baseball gods would reward my devotion to the game. All I wanted to do . . . was play.

Johnny and I made the trade—and the games began. I had a summer's worth of stale bubble gum and the assurance of playing baseball. I hit .395 that year, 118 home runs and 254 RBIs. It was a career year.

Plus, Johnny was not without conscience and knew how to keep his pipeline greased. Whenever there was an extra Twinkie that year, I got it. When he was allowed to take someone to the drive-in, I got the invite. And then there was the gum. He was true to his word on his end of the trade and I had chew all season long. *What is that white dust they use to cover the gum?*

And then, in late July, taking the two bucks I got for cutting Mr. Wallace's yard, I made the trek to Boardman Drug and bought more cards. Snagged a Hank Aaron card, too. The year he broke Babe Ruth's record.

Not even Johnny tried to negotiate for that one.

Part of what we learned, understood, and acted upon in those days, perhaps not on a conscious level, was the notion that no possession was as important as playing. We learned that "having" is not nearly as pleasing as "experiencing."

When I sense myself holding onto the baseball cards of my life, at the expense of playing baseball, I remember that spring and summer of my youth. It helps me to be more willing to trade for stale bubble gum.

Sand Scripts

Compromises
should never be
compromising.

"I Call," "Do Over," & "Ollie-Ollie-in-Free"

Of integrity, second chances, and absolution

We learned that we could make almost any reasonable assertion, condition, and/or change to a rule of a game if we added "I call!" to the end of the statement. The key was *reasonable*. We did have to lobby for consensus, another skill we gained from playing neighborhood ball.

"No tag-backs, no calling time, and no faking injuries when you're about to be caught—I call!"

"Nixon Street is foul territory—I call!"

"We're playing winners today. It's make-it-take-it—I call!"

"No noogies in the pile-ups. You noogie a guy in a pile-up and you lose a touchdown—I call!"

It didn't always go smoothly, this declarative act of setting gaming conditions. We'd have horrendous arguments and kids would storm off the field never to return (that day). Another fact of neighborhood games is you had to learn to "get over it" when you were wronged or injured. What drove this reconciliation of emotions and actions was, as often as not, our drive to play. We got graduate level training in counseling and negotiating right there on the fields of play in our neighborhoods.

The thing about making an "I call" was that you had to live with the consequences even if it worked against you. If you didn't have that kind of integrity, you never got to make an "I call" again.

Another of our great inventions was the unilateral,

unequivocal genius of the "do-over." "Do-overs" were kind of like mulligans and we only got one per round. A do-over was that time when conditions allowed for us to repeat an action without penalty and with equal opportunity for success as what came on the initial attempt.

"Ollie-Ollie-in-Free" was different, and a bit more sophisticated. It was the universal call of amnesty, the pardon without consequence, the get-out-of-jail-free card, and it had to be treated with the reverence it was due. It was the phrase you cried in the middle of a round of Ghost-in-the-Graveyard or Kick-the-Can or Hide-and-Seek when you wanted everyone to come back to the base because either someone had called the round off or someone had committed an infraction so egregious that the round must be replayed.

The upside of the Ollie-Ollie-in-Free was anyone already captured was released back into the game, without penalty or prejudice.

The downside of it came if you had found an excellent hiding place and now, being summoned by the call every player must obey, you had to step from your clandestine cubby and reveal your whereabouts to everyone else. It was a moment of truth to call Ollie-Ollie-in-Free; like the boy who cried "wolf," you never wanted to abuse that call. It was too important to our nighttime games. It was used if someone's parents were calling him in, if a younger contestant was thought to be missing, or if you couldn't find any of your hidden friends and you thought they had all gone inside and left you to roam the darkening night in search of them while they looked at you and laughed from inside their homes. Not that that ever happened to me.

Ollie-Ollie-in-Free was not just a shout-out; it was part of a sacred code, never to be abused.

We need more Ollie-Ollie-in-Frees in our lives as adults because while it's true that real life doesn't give us many "Do-overs," Ollie-Ollie-in-Frees should be dispensed to us, our families, friends, and loved ones with childlike abandon.

Sand Scripts

The success of all
future compromises
is determined by
the integrity of
the present one.

Under the Shade of the Dogwood Tree

Your yard – your game – your rules

In our neighborhoods, the soup du jour was always stone soup.

Someone brought a ball.

Someone brought a bat.

Sometimes we shared ball gloves.

Someone brought the board game.

Someone brought treats.

Someone's parents let us sit in their yard.

Together we merged our assets so we wouldn't end up just sitting on them.

The one standing rule was this: if it was your yard, you made the rules. If yours was the predominant piece of equipment, you owned the filibuster.

Richie may have had the best playground ball in the neighborhood, but Barbie's driveway had the biggest apron and sported four perfect squares. So we played four square in Barbie's driveway where her rules disallowed "spinners." But since it was Richie's playground ball, "atomic spikers" were allowed.

Eileen's sidewalk was the best place for hopscotch, an older section of the block still replete with the slate sidewalk that allowed for the stones to slide when you threw them. However, Becky usually had sidewalk chalk, so we'd play hopscotch in front of Eileen's house on a board drawn by Becky's chalk, which meant you were allowed to lean forward when you attempted to throw your stone in the number ten box—but if any part of the stone touched a line, the throw was no good.

Perhaps the most striking example of the power of this rule was presented to my conscience when, as a newly married couple, my wife and I decided to pass one evening playing monopoly. At that time it was the closest we were going to come to owning real estate.

She retrieved her childhood monopoly game from the back of our closet; I was stunned to see the mint condition of her game—now nearly twenty years old. The money was crisp and nearly brand new; the property deeds still had a sheen to them, and the board itself was as pristine as the day it rolled off the assembly line.

"Wow, so you guys didn't play with this much, then, aye?"

"We played with it all the time . . . but we played by *my* rules."

My quizzical, if not shocked, expression begged more explanation, which my wife supplied.

"Well, I had the only Monopoly game on the block. Margie had the best yard to play in on a summer's day; the grass thick as a carpet and manicured to perfection. Her dad was fanatical about their lawn. They also had the biggest dogwood tree you ever saw—and it gave shade like an umbrella over that lush lawn. So, on hot summer afternoons, we'd sit on her yard, and I'd run home and get my Monopoly game. We were allowed to sit on her grass if we didn't pull at it—and they were allowed to play with my Monopoly game if they agreed to certain rules."

"Which were?"

"Well, first, you couldn't curl the money in your fist like some people do. My rule was the money was gently tucked under the edge of the board and, when retrieving it, you 'plucked it' as though you were sneaking a potato chip from the bowl.

"The deeds stayed with me—I'd arrange them according

to who owned them, but they never left my possession.

"Lastly, you air counted when you moved."

"Air counted?"

"Yes, air counted. There was no need to tap the board with your piece to count out the moves. I had them count in the air and then set their piece on the spot where they landed."

"And they consented to this?"

"Hey, Margie had the shade . . . but I had the game."

Sand Scripts

The best compromises
create a middle ground
that isn't too muddy
to play on.

Visioneer

Hear the Voices

God Doesn't Hit Curve Balls

If I Make this it Means

Visioneer

When you change the way you look at things—
the things you look at change.
—Dr. Wayne Dyer

I am a huge fan of the emerging notion that our thoughts greatly impact the physical realities of our lives. The burgeoning body of evidence is as amazing as it is encouraging. This precept resonates so strongly with me because it directly reflects the experiences of my life. When you can look down a narrow city street that allows parking on both sides, when you can walk from one stop sign to the other on the roofs of cars and *still see* in that same street the outline of a baseball field, you've pretty well mastered the art of *see it; believe it; achieve it.*

They say that as you dream, your body has the same physiological responses it would have if the same events occurred while you are awake. It is unable to distinguish the events of your mind from the notion of physical or mental "reality." I think our neighborhood play was only one degree of separation from this intrinsic truth.

As we imagined ourselves as the Michael Jordan, Tiger Woods, or Peyton Manning's of our day, as we mimicked their accomplishments in our side yards—our brains were releasing the endorphins and dopamine that gave us the rush of accomplishment and experience that in the physical world would be well beyond our reach.

The point of connection between our visioneered

experiences and our ultimate realities was crystallized for me by a childhood friend, Bobby DiMiosso. Bobby and I ran into each other later in life, and I invited him and his wife to our home for dinner.

We had called him "Bobby D." as kids, but the truth is a more fitting nickname would have been "Eeyore." Poor Bobby always worried, fretted, and predicted doom.

"Think our moms will find out?"

Every time he said that, they did.

"I don't think we're gonna make it before dark."

Every time he said that, we never did.

"I bet we don't get picked."

Every time he said that . . .

So after several hours of visiting and coming to know more about each others' adult lives, Bobby turned to me and said, "Wow, it looks like your life turned out just like you always imagined it would."

Hear the Voices

Your internal play-by-play voice will determine your performance and—your destiny

On Wednesday, March 16, 1977, at ten thirty in the morning, in Mr. Kent's tenth-grade English class, I came face-to-face with a monster I had dreaded and dodged for the previous 9.66 years of my academic life. I had vexed my demon at every turn, at times out-running him, at times out-maneuvering him, at times feigning illness, and, yes, at times just outright deceiving him through verbal distortions of the truth (I lied). And who was this dreaded ogre who dogged my every academic moment?

Public speaking.

In a recent survey, fear of public speaking ranked number one on things people fear the most. Burning to death was number four.

As much as we hear our voices in the unending internal dialogue of our thoughts—something about hearing the physical projection of our voice sends most of us cringing in a fear even Stephen King can't reproduce.

I had built the moment into something of a guillotine of self-esteem because of my spasmodic dysphonia. Not having control of the muscles that move air across my larynx is a tough enough challenge when I am calm and relaxed. When I am nervous, the resulting spastic movement of those muscles makes my speech sound like I am choking, gasping, and more in search of my last breath than articulating a message.

In order to help his students deal with this fear, Mr. Kent had crafted a maniacal web of consequences if you were not "present" when it came time to do your speech. If you were absent when he "randomly" called on you to take the podium, your assignment changed from a three-minute speech to a six-minute speech. If you missed that speech, you got a twelve-minute assignment. If you missed that, you'd be giving your speech to the senior English class across the hall. Oh yeah, Mr. Kent was a genius. I question his motives though. If the goal was to get us over the fear, why did he have to make the selection random? Methinks he may have enjoyed administering the tough love of making us speak publicly.

I went all the way through Monday and Tuesday's classes doing stomach crunches every time a name was called. I think there are probably still finger indents in the desk I occupied.

Then it happened—725,760 seconds into my school career—the moment had arrived. I can still hear the call of doom.

"Next up to wile, entertain, and otherwise enlighten us with his speech . . . we have . . . Mr. Porter."

I swallowed hard and rose to stand on feet that had no blood in them. I walked with legs that had suddenly turned to columns of granite. I saw the second hand of the clock moving with the slow, dispassionate exactness of an executioner sharpening his ax. I saw the steady, reassuring gaze of my best friend in the back row, half of his demeanor encouraging, the other half wondering if he should move forward to catch me if I passed out.

Inside my thoughts, a set of voices had whirled into motion to give me the messages that might serve to get me through this moment.

It wasn't the voice of my mother telling me how precious and special I was.

It wasn't my brothers admonishing me to "suck it up" and "be a man."

It wasn't the voice of my father rendering a compelling rendition of the little engine who thought he could.

It wasn't even Bobby Darin singing, "Oops there goes another rubber tree plant."

It was the voices of sportscasters whose play-by-play and color commentary calls served as the narrators of my internal dialogue. As I walked down the tiered steps of our auditorium-style classroom, to the outside world it may have seemed I was thinking, "Oh no, I can't do this; I can't do this. Ohmygod, I have to do this. . . ." but inside, that's not what I was doing at all.

I was hearing the voices.

In this case the reigning sports event of the moment in my life was the annual NCAA basketball tournament known as "March Madness." It was the perfect balance point to the madness of the fear I felt for having to give a public speech.

"Well, John, this has turned into the epic classic we thought it would be. It's absolute bedlam hear at Pauley Pavilion on the campus of UCLA. Three ticks left on the clock, the Bruins down by a point, and Porter stepping to the free throw line. If he makes these two free throws, his Bruins win the NC2A championship— miss them, and they go home in second place. As he steps to the line—Kentucky calls a time out.

They're trying to put pressure on him. They want to give him a little time to think it over.

They're wasting their time. This young fella has ice in his veins. He is one cool customer under pressure.

He steps to the line, bounces the ball three times, spins it in his hands, he bends—eyes locked on the basket, here's the free throw, it's up, it's . . .

I gave the speech that day, bolstered by the encouragement of my best buddy in the back row hand signaling the time remaining and looking like a parent who knew the letters to your word in the spelling bee; I was encouraged by the looks of empathy from those who had given their speeches already, and comforted, oddly, by the abject horror in the eyes of those who had not—because at least my time had come and would soon pass.

I don't even recall the compliment Mr. Kent gave me as I returned to my seat, didn't hear the name of the next victim he had called out. No, I walked back to my seat, listening to the imagined adulations of tens of thousands of fans and my commentator appropriately marking the epic nature of my accomplishment.

"We've just witnessed one of the great clutch performances of all time! You talk about pressure—the entire weight of a basketball legacy on his shoulders, absolute mayhem in the arena, millions of viewers world-wide—and this scrappy youngster from northeast Ohio steps to the line and drains the bottom from the nets!"

We encouraged ourselves, borrowing the color commentary of those who called out the accomplishments of our favorite players, for it wasn't just their physical accomplishments we were trying to mimic. We sought to emulate our sports heroes as much for their calm under pressure, their stoicism, their persistence and their courage—as much as for any of their physical accomplishments, maybe more. No one could cauterize the moments as well as the commentators of the day; that's why we chose them to be the voice of our inner dialogue, especially when we were in tight spots. It added inspiration to the attempt and significance to the accomplishment. Let's face it, when you conquered a demon, rose up, and beat the odds, you wanted to have it galvanized for prosperity!

"He stole home base . . . he stole home base, seventh game of the World Series and he steals home base! How about that for the guts of a cat burglar!"

As I often tell my children, I grew up with an embarrassment of riches when it came to the music, movies, television, and sports heroes of my generation. We had the best of class everywhere we looked, and especially so with the sports commentators of our day. We had Curt Gowdy, "Dandy Don" Meredith, Pat Summerall, Dick Enberg, Lindsey Nelson, Jack Buck, Phil Rizzuto, Joe Garagiola, Keith Jackson, and of course, Howard Cosell, just to name a few. Their skills and talents galvanized the hours of practice turned to moments of glory with phrases like:

"Oh my!" and . . .

"Whoa Nellie! We got a real down-home donnybrook going on here!" and . . .

"Turn out the lights . . . the party's over," and . . .

"This one's hit waaaayyy back—GONE!" and . . .

"Dribble drive right side, pulls up for an eighteen-footer from the baseline—he shoots! He scores!"

We used these patented phrases to call out the start of our own games, chronicle the play-by-play, and otherwise annoy one another.

The ultimate narrator for our day was a man whose name none of us knew at the time, John Facenda. He, above all, was the voice rolling through the landscape of our thoughts as we reached for performance supremacy, as we strove to become legends in our own minds.

He was the voice of NFL Films.

He was the man who introduced us to such iconic phrases as "the frozen tundra of Lambeau Field"; "the mighty Steel Curtain defense of the vaunted Pittsburgh Steelers"; and, "the last of the great gunslingers."

He had the ability to tell a story in such a riveting way that we must have appeared like the Depression-era youth sitting around the radio listening to Orson Welles's rendition of the *War of the Worlds*. We weren't watching football highlights; we were watching *theater*.

Every Saturday in the fall, we would gather in the Paressis' family room at 1:45 p.m. This allowed fifteen minutes before the 2:00 p.m. broadcast—enough time for Steve Paressi to argue with his sisters, chase them out of the room, throw piles of dirty clothes off the family room couch, while his brother Dave secured the much-anticipated snack food and we looked for a place to sit among the rubble. With all this accomplished, a hush would fall over the room as the *NFL Game of the Week* flickered onto the television set (the Paressis, while they did not have maid service, had the best television in the neighborhood—we knew things like that in our day).

Before there was endless ESPN, Fox, satellite coverage, and replays of every activity in sports; before we knew what our heroes ate, what they drove, how many rooms their mansions had, who they were dating, and what their agent looked like, there were only two main sources for highlights: half-time of the Monday Night Football game, where the fastest two minutes in sports was born, and the NFL Game of the Week. Since you were not always assured of being awake for the halftime of Monday Night Football, Saturday afternoon's Game of the Week was not to be missed.

We would sit in complete silence, our eyes and ears drinking in every sound, every cut of music, every slow-motion sequence, every epic narration, because immediately following the show, and for the remainder of that week, we would be heading to the fields to reenact everything we had seen and heard.

Slow-motion highlights were the staple of our sports fantasies. They allowed all of us to believe we could make the plays our heroes were making. We couldn't play the game at the level or the speed of the pros, but when you slowed it down, we all could see the dance steps of the brutal ballet sports could sometimes be.

You could see the quarterback taking the seven-step drop back; you saw the running back pumping his shoulders and legs with piston-like proficiency; the wide receiver whose reach was *not* exceeding his grasp; the linebacker closing in for the tackle and the safety zeroing in for a bone-crushing shot.

After the painfully brief thirty-minute episode, we would head for our ball field where the reenactments would begin. We all played the commentator and the player. What a sight we must have been to those driving by. A handful of kids, all moving in what appeared to be a synchronized purpose, like a walk-through at a play or Hollywood production where the director was organizing the next stunt.

The only thing we couldn't figure out was how to throw a pass and make the ball move in slow motion.

Much to the amusement and occasional bemusement of my wife, I still "hear the voices." They couch accomplishments, celebrate successes, and buffet the failures. They transform the mundane to the sublime. They infuse enthusiasm into the ordinary and underscore the magic of the moment.

The accomplishments we garner in overcoming personal demons, life-station challenges, and obstacles of this world should be immortalized by a baritone narrator reminding the rest of us of their significance. Indeed, we need to be reminded, at times, that the grandeur of the attempt is worth the sting of failure.

Sand Scripts

Every life deserves
to have its highlights
narrated by a
Hall of Fame broadcaster.

God Doesn't Hit Curve Balls

Learning the fine art of self-reliance

God doesn't hit curve balls. The good news is: he doesn't *throw* them either. At least not in little league games, disguised as the opposing pitcher staring you down in your moment of truth.

I have a friend, Ron Schmidt, a very accomplished man. He owns an accounting firm and is civic activist, baseball coach, advocate, veteran of numerous Boston Marathons, Rotarian—just an incredible guy. We were at lunch discussing "neighborhood days" and lessons learned when he gave an insightful commentary about a pivotal moment in his childhood.

"I grew up in Middlesboro, Kentucky: classic small town in middle America in the early sixties. For us, baseball was everything. I was a good player, too—fielded well, base running was above average, and I could hit. Well, the point of demarcation between being a good little league player and a guy who could make pony league level was the ability to hit a curve ball. And I struggled. And I struggled.

"I remember standing in the batter's box facing a kid who could throw a wicked curve ball. I was praying, I mean pleading with God to let me get a hit. I got behind in the count and I increased my pleading. The pitcher rocks back and this nasty, nasty curve ball sends me down swinging.

"As I was walking back to the dugout, the revelation came

119

to me, 'God doesn't hit curve balls.' Mind you, it didn't shake my faith, nor did I feel abandoned by God; it's just that at that moment I realized God gives you the gifts, but *you* have to develop them. In that self-actualizing moment, I learned the concept of self-reliance. And do you want to know something? After that moment, I couldn't *not* hit a curve ball."

Long before I had occasion to "pray to the porcelain god" as an errant college freshmen experiencing the excesses of fraternity parties, I prayed to the sports gods, Rawlings, Spalding, and Wilson.

"Please don't let him hit the ball toward me."

"Lord, I know I'm wide open on the wing—but please don't let him see me."

"Dear God, this is Danny. I'm going to heave up a free throw in a moment here. Please let it go in! Please let it go in! Please let it go in!" (It had to be a thrice-mentioned plea. Why—I don't know. Perhaps an unconscious reference to the Holy Trinity.)

When you consider the vernacular of organized sports, it's hard to fault a child for asking—nay, pleading—for divine intervention. Here is a sampling of the kinds of statements I heard while attempting to play little league baseball.

"Okay, Danny, get ready. This guy is a real flamethrower! Yessiree, baby. This guy is bringing heat!"

"*Excuse me, Coach, would those be actual flames? I think I'm allergic to flames. I get heat rashes really easily. Could Bobby bat for me today?*"

"Dig in, Danny. Get set in that batter's box. This guy has a CANNON for an arm!"

"*Time out, Mr. Umpire. . . . Sorry, Coach—did you say 'Cannon,' 'cause I gotta tell ya, I don't usually stand in front of weapons of mass destruction. I don't like loud noises. I don't even go to firework shows.*"

Trust me, I would have benefitted from a baseball being the size of a cannonball, but I really didn't need for it to be hurling at my head at a speed of a hundred feet per second.

In the field it wasn't much better.

"Awright, Danny, heads up now. This guy swings a mean axe!"

I was playing third base at the time—street smart enough to realize I was in the direct line of fire if that "axe" slipped from yonder batter's hand. My dad was a New York City kid, so the only thing I knew about an axe was watching the opening of Daniel Boone where he splits an entire tree by throwing an axe at it. Somehow I saw myself as that tree.

"Coach, maybe Ryan should play third base. I tend to bleed a lot when injured."

My coaches emphasized the use of my body a great deal, not so much out of respect for my considerable ability as much as from the notion of expendability.

On defense they often told me: "Keep your body in front of the ball, Danny."

"What do you mean?"

"Get low to the ground; square your shoulders. You want to make your body like a backstop behind the catcher—so if the ball gets past your glove, see, it will hit your body and you'll stop it."

The only phrase I heard in that statement was, *"hit your body."* And so I prayed the ball would not come in my direction.

My little league coach, now he *did* know the Teddy Roosevelt quote, "Do what you can, with what you have, where you are." He sized up my athletic ability and immediately began coaching me on how to "lean into the pitch, Danny" so that I would be hit by the pitch and thus be awarded a trip to first base. It was the only way I ever got on base.

I wish I had come to Ron's epiphany as a youngster. It may well have saved my immortal soul. I have grave concerns that my moment of truth at the pearly gates is going to have more to do with my broken bargains than my un-negotiated mistakes. In the heat of sports contests, I made a lot of deals with God, and I am fairly certain in his scoring of the game I may lead the league in errors when it came to holding up my end of the deal.

St. Peter: "It says here if we allowed you to grow to be six feet tall, you were going to volunteer every Saturday to wash windows at church."

Me: "I'm six-three, and I was really hoping to be just the six feet—so I felt the term of the request hadn't actually been met."

St. Peter: "I see. It says here if you passed freshman algebra, you were going to spend time visiting Mrs. Crochett, the elderly woman in your neighborhood."

Me: "Yeah, see, about that . . . every time I went by to visit her, it seemed she was sleeping."

St. Peter: "It was usually eleven thirty p.m. She was eighty-three—of course she was sleeping. Running under her bedroom window while playing kick the can does not meet our standard for 'stopping by to visit'."

Me: "My bad on that one, that's for sure."

St. Peter: "Shall we even discuss the dates you were granted in exchange for the work you were going to do in the soup kitchens?"

Me: "What would you say if I told you the soup kitchen was in a tough part of town and I was really afraid to go there?"

St. Peter: "Well . . . I guess I'd say . . . 'go to hell'."

There's a flamethrower I don't want to face.

Sand Scripts

It's a great day
when you discover
you can count on
yourself.

If I Make this it Means . . .

Quarterly projections are not as reliable as shooting foul shots

I think it was Peter Drucker, renowned management consultant, who said that the best way to predict the future is to create it. We were forever using our skills in "visioneering" to create our future. We had no use for Ouija boards, tarot cards, horoscopes, or fortune-tellers. In fact, we could teach a thing or two to corporate business analysts who create quarterly business projections. We had a lock-tight method for predicting the future in a way that created it. It started always with the phrase, *"If I make this it means . . ."*

The "make this" part always involved some attempt to land an object in a certain spot. Be it a foul shot, a three-pointer, a football tossed to a precise target, a rock hitting a stop sign, or simply throwing a wad of paper in a trash can—the idea was, if we were successful in hitting a target with our projectile of choice, a certain and unalterable consequence ensued thereafter. The powerful undertone of this ritual was that we believed the consequence of our prediction!

I remember standing on the foul line of our driveway basketball court (we used a crack in the concrete as our "foul line," and to this day I couldn't tell you if it was ten feet from the hoop or the regulation fifteen feet), ritualistically bouncing the ball three times before attempting a foul shot, and whispering on the air, *"If I make this shot, it means I will make the freshman basketball team."*

The shot would clank off the rim and fall unsuccessfully to the asphalt with a thud of doom. I would retrieve it, return to the foul line, and say, *"If I make **seven out of ten**, it means I will make the basketball team."* The times I made those shots I'd continue through the rest of my day with an air of expectancy—I had created a vision of a certain future and I lived in excited, peaceful, and blissful anticipation of that future.

As I aged, I used the process for more important predications. "If I make this shot, I will go to prom with Alison McKeyes. . . ."

Alison was apparently not tuned into the universe's vibrations and never got the message that she was supposed to respond in the affirmative; but, hey, the process helped me build the courage to ask.

This technique was also used as the full-proof goad when one or more of your neighborhood playmates were not up for games on a particular day. Maybe you went to call them for the day's games and contests, and they just weren't feeling like running wide-open that particular day.

You'd all be sitting around someone's stoop, idle and unable to find a common venue for engaging in a game. So you'd pick up the first projectable object you could find, choose a target—the striking of which could only be accomplished by an individual in total synchronization with the universe, and therefore someone who should be listened to—and you would boldly state the future that would unfold should you strike said target. It was as if we believed hitting the target set in motion a sequence of cosmic dominos that we could never again set upright.

"If I hit the stop sign, it means we're playing Frisbee tag and everyone has to play."

You would get your detractors, hedonists who flew in the face of cosmic truths, and they'd say things like, "No, I ain't playing if you hit Mars with a marshmallow."

So you'd have to layer consequence onto your action.

"If I hit the stop sign, it means we're playing Frisbee tag and everyone has to play. Anyone who doesn't play is saying he'd rather kiss Jenny O'Bannon than play Frisbee tag and therefore must kiss Jenny O'Bannon. "

Everyone would leap to their feet, in dire anticipation of the assault on the stop sign—and let me tell you, if you tinged the target, everyone was in for the game. There are some unnatural forces in the universe any prudent playster just didn't mess with.

There was, however, a time when I carried it too far.

My older brother Tom was busy washing his old gold Ford XL fastback in our driveway, and I was trying to get him to consent to play all-time quarterback for our brand of side-yard spring football. It was a stretch-goal from the get-go. Tom was getting ready for a date that night and his mind was a million miles from sandlot football. Who could blame him? He was a senior in high school, atop the sports and social world, having just smashed the school record in the mile, and travelling everywhere with the swoon-inducing Becky on his arm.

It started innocuously enough.

"If I hit the mailbox with this rock, you have to play football with us; and, if you don't, it means that *I* am faster than *you.*"

Now the mailbox was maybe thirty feet away, as big as a breadbox, and I had a rock the size of a tennis ball. The degree of difficulty for this shot was (given that I was throwing it) about 2.5; for anyone else, it was like a 1.2.

That one was so lame it didn't even warrant a look from Tom, who turned up his Three Dog Night eight-track and kept washing his car. I had to reach a bit further.

"If I can throw this rock into the birdbath in Mrs. Auggie's yard, you have to play football with us, or it means you eat toe jam for breakfast."

Mrs. Auggie's front yard was maybe as far as the mailbox; the inviting diameter of her birdbath made it an easier shot than it may have seemed otherwise. Still, it demanded just the right touch. Degree of difficulty: 6.6. This one at least netted a response from Tom.

"First of all, birdbrain, if you're off even a little, and my money's on that, you're gonna bust the Auggies' picture window and the old man's gonna jam more than his toe up your ass. . . ."

I was making progress. I had reeled him into open dialogue on this subject. Then he changed the game, elevated the stakes, and hurt my pride by throwing down a gauntlet.

"Does this *ever* work for you? 'Cause I gotta tell ya, you suck at this."

My fellas were cackling with delight on the verbal dissing I had taken. I went into a mode that had me detached from the physical universe. Tight lipped and pride stinging, I called out an incantation to the universe.

"I hit the stop sign at the corner of North Broadway and McLaughlin, it means you play football with us, until I say we're done, or it means you're admitting Becky is the biggest bow-wow in the city."

First of all, it would be a blind throw. Between the pine trees that shot up forty feet at the end of our driveway and the maples in Johnny O.'s yard, you couldn't even *see* the stop sign at the corner of North Broadway and McLaughlin. Secondly, it had to be a good thirty to forty yards away. With me as the one attempting this shot, the degree of difficulty was easily ten to the tenth power.

Cue the music for the OK Corral. Clint Eastwood never mustered a stare like the one Tom was giving me at that moment. I turned like a directionally challenged discus thrower and let loose my assault on destiny.

It was like there was a tractor beam emanating from the stop sign to the rock—we all stood watching its trajectory over the Johnny's maples trees as though we were watching a Jack Nicklaus drive. When it cleared the maples easily, there was a pregnant pause in our collective group, the realization that the rock actually might "have a chance."

I can still close my eyes and hear the clank of stone against tin. To this day I truly believe my buddy, Donny Marshall, threw a rock from a different grassy knoll. Regardless, the striking of the stone to the sign was akin to the tolling of the bell of doom.

Time stood still. The universe awaited Tom's response. Was he going to play all-time quarterback or admit he was dating Benji.

It took me a millisecond to understand he wasn't doing either. He launched himself over the trunk of his beloved fastback like Bart Connor off a pommel horse. I took off in the only direction that gave me a chance—counting on my knowledge of Johnny's yard, my immediate strategy was to lead him around their house, lose him in their arbor vitae hedge, and duck back into our house, where I hoped my mommy was present.

He caught me before the first turn around Johnny's garage. To the raucous laughter of my turncoat friends, he started his defiance of the cosmos by giving me a little dose of "grassy back," a sadistic little practice of dragging an individual bare-backed across a grassy patch, yielding an itching sensation that renders poison ivy a sneeze by comparison.

With this completed, he hoisted me fireman-carry style over his shoulders. In spite of all my "I-take-it-backs" uttered as I laughed and cried, he was determined to administer his own karmic consequences for the insult hurled at his beloved Becky.

What happened next is still a blur to me. In motions as deft as any championship rodeo cowboy, he threw me on my belly in the middle of the dirt patch that was home plate in our front yard, tied my hands behind my back and my shoelaces to my belt loops so I looked like a human rocking horse, or a seal awaiting a beach ball on my nose, and proceeded to take the garden hose that he had been using to wash his car and soak the entire area around me until I was a rocking horse stuck in the mud.

My fellas were doubled over in laughter and probably wetting themselves at the scene. Tom's proclamation to them sealed my fate for the next several hours.

"He who helps him *joins* him."

I lay in that mud for hours.

My dad came home from work around six. Being one of four boys born to a man who used to tie his brother's pants and socks in knots because his brother always slept late and was always in a panic to prepare for school meant the man understood male sibling dynamics. He took one look at me as he exited his car and calmly and detachedly asked: "Lose a bet?"

"Kinda."

"Learn anything?"

"Kinda."

"What is it I'm always telling you?"

"Don't let my alligator mouth overload my canary ass."

"Good man. Now clean up and don't be late for dinner."

There'd be no help from my dad, who chuckled and went about his way. It was my sisters who came to my rescue. They functioned like Amnesty International in fraternal disputes such as this one.

Yep—that's the day I learned a new level of respect for cosmic forces and karma. Such principles are not to be messed with idly. Their justice is unequivocal and exacting.

As of this writing, Tom and Becky have been married for thirty-five years.

I'm still apologizing.

Sand Scripts

Never allow
the realization of
your dreams
to be determined by
something as fickle
as fate.

Persist

Two out, bottom of the Ninth

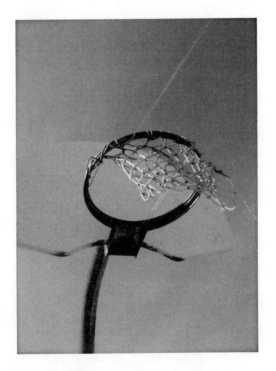

The Best of Infinity

The One-Point Difference

Persist

*Every block of stone has a statue inside of it,
and it is the sculptor's job
to discover it.*
—*Michelangelo*

I love the art of the sports debate for two primary reasons: firstly, you can never be proven definitively wrong, and secondly, it gives non-athletes something to do with their time. An endless smorgasbord awaits those with an appetite for feasting on the fare of debating sports accomplishments.

Who's the greatest quarterback of all time?

Which team carved out the greatest dynasty?

Name the top fifty athletes, all sports considered, of all time.

I enter every dialog, participate in every poll, and ponder every question—for the exercise of showing what I have observed of sports over the years.

There is, however, one sports debate I never enter. It's the one that considers the question: Should athletes be considered as role models? I never enter the debate for two primary reasons. First, it's a moot point—of course they are role models. Once you step on a stage as large as professional sports, you are by definition "modeling a role." Your actions in modeling that role may be judged as good, bad, or indifferent; but, like it or not, you're a professional athlete—you're a role model. The more important question isn't whether or not professional athletes should be considered role models, rather, what is happening in a young person's life that they choose to emulate one role model over another.

The second reason I never enter the debate is that to do so would be disrespectful to the role models of my youth. Part of the cornucopia of blessings that was my youth was the chance I had to model my behavior after some of the luminaries of sports character. I grew up knowing of Roberto Clemente and his work in Latin America. I watched in awe as John Cappelletti won the Heisman Trophy and then turned and gave it to his brother, Joey, who was dying of leukemia. I was part of the generation that watched *Brian's Song*, the Gale Sayers/Brian Piccolo story unfold. Of course there were problems in sports in those days—but they paled in comparison to the rich human drama unfolding within the stories of these sports figures and the manner in which they used their celebrity.

While these Maslowian peak experiences inspired me greatly, my sports hero role model was a quiet southern gentleman whose rugged physical toughness and determination called the beat by which I marched through the day-to-day battles with multifocal dystonia and became the beacon by which I navigated one of the most difficult stretches of my life.

Kudos to his sons for making it to the professional level, and it may well be that Peyton goes down in history as the greatest to ever play quarterback (there's one of the sports debates again), but like all old timers, I favor the original, the vintage, the classic Manning—the one my sisters came to call "St. Archie."

Archie Manning was the quarterback of the New Orleans Saints during a time period in their history when they were woeful. They went entire seasons winning only one game and seldom competing for victory in the others. At one point they were so bad their fans called them the "Aints" and wore brown bags over their heads when attending the games.

So how does an otherwise die-hard ten-year-old Cleveland

Browns fan living on the shores of the North Coast come to choose the quarterback from the Big Easy as his primary role model? If I had to sum up succinctly what it represented to me at that moment and ever since, I would say is thusly: it was his *dignified and courageous persistence.*

At the time I discovered Archie Manning, I was ten years old and just coming into the throes of having to come to terms with the fact I was "different" . . . and that difference had me viewing myself as being lesser than others. Multifocal dystonia was neither widely nor easily diagnosed in those days. I remember many a time when I was about to catch a pass and my hands abducted, the sports-talk equivalent of turning to stone. Or as I'd be about to sprint off first in pursuit of second base, my legs would spasm, and I'd be tripping over obstacles in my path that didn't actually exist.

Absent an obvious malady, I was labeled a "spaz" and went through the jaunts and taunts most of our lives experience at one point, or for one reason or another. By the dawn of fourth grade, I was facing the gap in my sports abilities compared to my peers on a daily basis. Lunch, recess, and gym became the demons that haunted my waking hours and many of my sleeping ones, as well. Add to the mix a hyper-macho male teacher who frequently enjoyed a chiding remark at my expense and you get the picture.

I remember the first time I saw Archie Manning. We had just gotten a brand new color television, and Dad had splurged on cable for the first time ever. For us, it was the equivalent of HDTV. It was a Saturday afternoon when the installation was finally complete and the first program that flickered on the screen was the vaunted NFL Game of the Week. For some inexplicable reason, because I don't think either team was a premier team, the game featured the Detroit Lions versus the New Orleans Saints.

The program kept keying on how the Detroit Lions' defense was punishing the young Saints' quarterback. In replay after replay, juxtaposed to a daunting music bed, they showed Archie Manning being thrown to the ground. Each time he was sacked, he rose quickly back to his feet and went about the next play. Occasionally he would need to stop and adjust a shoulder pad, pull up a sock, or reset his jaw—but always he sprung back to his feet. One video montage showed him being sacked seven or eight times in a row, vicious, crushing hits. The montage ended with Archie being momentarily stung by a particularly tough hit; he rolled over and rose to one knee, paused to gather himself, then rose like a prizefighter struggling to beat a ten-count.

I decided right then and there that I was going to be Archie Manning. I was going to rise after every hit; every time my dystonia "sacked" me, I was going to spring to my feet and try again. And even if the "hit" was exceptionally vicious, I would not tarry on my back. I would rise slowly to one knee if that be all the courage I could muster. Come what may, I was never going down and out for the count. I had a hero, a star to navigate by, and a role model.

In those days you couldn't easily follow your favorite sports team. Heck, barring the radio, it wasn't all that easy to follow your local sports team, let alone a franchise from another city. Add to it that your favorite player was on a franchise that was a perennial basement dweller, and you may as well have been charting the movements of one of America's Most Wanted. News or images of my hero were hard to come by. My dad had picked up on my reasoning for liking Archie Manning as much as I did, so he broke with family rule and allowed me to watch the end of the second NFL game on Sunday with the hopes of picking up a score or some news of how Archie had faired that day. As hard as it was to pull in images of your favorite sports team, the marketing of NFL merchandise was still in its infancy, and the only source for anything with Archie's image or a Saints logo was the Sears annual Christmas wish catalog.

I started using the play-by-play voice of John Facenda

when life set me back because of my disease. As I walked back to the group in gym class, having flubbed another athletic drill or exercise, and listening to my teacher cackle his "C'mon, Porter, are you a man or a mouse?" in my mind I was Archie Manning going back to the huddle and John Facenda was lauding my courage.

"The pounding, grueling hits just keep coming his way, but Archie Manning rises where most others would fall—he, with the courage and determination of a lone warrior battling unbeatable odds . . ."

He was, in the opinion of many experts then and now, a great player on a bad team—and yet, he never complained, never demanded to be traded. He did his job, worked hard, kept his head up—and kept going. All laudable qualities, but it was one act alone that elevated him to be dubbed "St. Archie" by my sisters.

It was the fall of 1973. After undergoing a year and a half of neurological testing that was attempting to decipher the nature of my physical challenges, and having gone through several experiments with different medicines that left me feeling mostly lethargic, the lack of a clear diagnosis led to the concern that I might have a brain tumor which was causing the maladies I was experiencing. I was admitted to Cleveland's Rainbow Babies and Children's Hospital where I would undergo additional testing, inclusive of a neuro-encephalogram, a test that was a precursor to CAT Scans and would have me knocked flat on my back for several weeks.

The doctors explained the process in an attempt to prepare my mother. It began with a spinal tap, and once the needle was in the spinal canal, air was introduced that traveled into the cranium, filled in the spaces around the brain, and allowed for x-rays that would help determine if, in fact, tumors were present in the brain. Once introduced into the cranium, the air did its job. Except then it had to go somewhere, which meant pressure so intense it was literally enough to knock you on your back. In the first few days after the procedure, simply lifting my head off my pillow was enough to induce vomiting.

Hearing the nature of the procedure and fearing the potential of the diagnosis, my family and extended family whirled into motion, producing support, encouragement, and the love that carried me through. In particular, my Aunt Maureen placed a call to the New Orleans Saints and explained both my medical situation and my dedication to their team and their quarterback.

The first week of testing was so easy. I was enjoying the week off school it had provided me. The Saints had beaten the Redskins the Sunday I entered the hospital, and I was certain the testing was going to cure me, so I was riding an incredible high.

Then came the neuro-encephalogram. I remember the discomfort of the needle. I remember vomiting profusely as the dizziness began its relentless parade in my skull. I remember praying it all be over. I remember them wheeling me back to my room and my vision coming into focus on my dad, who had a look of vulnerability I had never before seen on his face. Seeing he had my conscious attention, he whispered, "Guess what, Dano? You got a little mail today." His voice was course in the way a strong man sounds when emotions are overtaking him. "I'm just going to read you part of it; you can open everything that came once you're feeling better, okay?"

Not waiting my answer, he began reading:

Dear Danny,

We received word from your aunt that you're one of our biggest fans and that Archie Manning is your favorite player. We also learned of the medical challenges you are facing. When we told Archie of your situation, he wanted you to have the enclosed gifts to let you know we're all thinking of you and pulling for your complete recovery. We need our number one Cleveland fan back in the game and rooting for us!

Best Wishes,

The New Orleans Saints

I am one who will tell you the mind plays a huge role in healing the body. For the days that followed, Archie's autographed picture stayed on my hospital nightstand. As soon as I could sit up in bed, I opened the rest of what they had sent: it was a full-blown replica uniform of Archie's—jersey, helmet, pants, and all. The old gold and black number 8 jersey was never off my body for the month of recovery that followed. The gesture has never left my mind, nor my heart.

That's when he became for my sisters, my family, and for me "St. Archie," for he provided heavenly inspiration to a young boy struggling to find a self-image amid the effects of the silent prankster who had taken up permanent residence in his body.

That inspiration came from the way he modeled the role he had been given and is a quality I still work to emulate—*dignified, courageous perseverance.*

Sand Scripts

The act of kindness
you offer
May not seem like much
to you,
but remember—
you are not the one
who decides its value.
That is done
by the one
who receives it.

Two out, bottom of the Ninth

It takes one thousand hours of preparation for one moment of glory

Have you seen these contraptions they've invented, the ones where you don a device that looks like welder's goggles and it allows you to enter a virtual universe wherein the action of the game appears three-dimensional? We saw them in action at the fair last year. People looking rather silly as we watched them bob, dodge, parry, and thrust into mid-air. They were seeing the images of the games on their private virtual screens. We were seeing them pantomime reality. Virtual Reality, they call it.

We did the same thing as kids. Only we had a different term for it. We called it "imagination." As you drove through our neighborhoods, you may have seen us playing ball in the streets, but I can assure you, in our minds, we were always at bat in Yankee Stadium. That patch of grass you saw us playing football on was always Lambeau field. And the rickety hoop barely attached to its backboard was always hanging from the rafters of Boston Garden.

There is a concept in sports today referred to as "muscle memory." It's a concept built on the premise that if we perform an athletic action enough times in practice (using proper form and technique) the motion will burn itself in our body's memory. In the split second reality of a sports moment, there is no time for conscious thought of what to do, for if you have to think about it, then the moment passes. By practicing thousands of times, when it comes time for the action to be performed in the reality of a moment, the body will simply take over, the muscles will remember what to do, and performance will be maximized.

I'm constantly telling my kids and the kids I coach in youth basketball that it's a thousand-to-one ratio. For every one moment of athletic accomplishment that is achieved, there were a thousand moments of practice that went into the act. The trick is, you don't think of it as practice, for few can pony up for that kind of grueling track. No, it wasn't practice in our day . . . it was play.

A friend of mine and I were pontificating on this notion of modern youth missing the point that skills development was ingeniously disguised as play in our day. For him, it was all about the crabapples.

"We lived on five acres on the edge of town—it was my old man's pride and joy. From the road, the place looked like a little corner of heaven. Five acres—a kid's paradise, right? Not so much. Three acres of woods, the house, the barn, and a crabapple orchard took up a lot of the land. One of our chores was to pick up the crabapples that fell so Dad could cut the grass around the trees a few times a year. So we'd head out there with five-gallon pails and gather up the fallen crabapples, and then we'd juice 'em in a game called *smash ball*.

"One of us would pitch the crabapples to the other, who would endeavor to smash them so hard they either carried into the woods or were obliterated on the spot. It was actually more fun when we were able to smash them, as opposed to homering them into the woods. Smashing them resulted in the juice of the apple going everywhere: on us, mostly on us, and the best shots covered the opposing pitcher with sticky, slimy remnants of a decaying crabapple.

"With every swing of the bat it was 'two outs, full count, loaded bases, bottom of the ninth, seventh game of the World

Series,'" he related with a laugh, and then an astonished memory: "I mean, really, we took it seriously, man—if you gave up that grand slam, you really felt like you had blown the World Series!"

Many a major leaguer will tell you similar stories of athletic acumen built up over countless hours of *practice* changed to *play* by the strength of our imagination.

My older brother, Tom, was forever concocting "drills" for me to do. He'd spend countless hours tossing me grounders and throwing "pop-ups" I needed to shag, all the while peppering the drill with the banter of the play-by-play man.

"There's a sharply hit ball up the middle, Porter lunges to his left, backhands the ball, whirls, and throws—two out!"

The addition of the play-by-play commentary added motivation and significance to the moment, lest our activity take on the dryness of rote practice. I see that as a limitation of organized sports. When you're slugging your way through hours of drills, the coach isn't adding the drama of a visioneered reality.

Another drill Tom gave me provided me access to one of the top ten highlights of my sandlot career. In those days, Spalding made a rubberized version of a hardball that was cheaper and less dangerous than the real McCoy. We seldom used it in full-fledged games because even I could launch one of those vulcanized puppies a country mile. It was best for games of five hundred, or five dollars, where one person would bat and the rest of us would field. Catching a fly ball earned you one hundred points, or a dollar; dropping it docked you a like amount. A one hopper was seventy-five, and two-hopper, fifty . . . anything rolling was twenty-five.

Tom took that Spalding wonder, and me, to Garfield Elementary one day in the spring after our first sandlot baseball game of the season. It was time for a little fielding practice, and Tom wanted to empower me to practice by myself.

"Okay, here's what I want you to do," he instructed me,

and as soon as he was assigning the task, I was all up and all in for completing it. "Don't wait for me or Kevin to be around to practice your fielding. Come up here and use this wall. You throw it hard and low to practice scooping grounders; you throw it belt high to practice catching liners; and you throw it as high as you can, still keeping a little mustard on it, so it forces you to run down high fly balls. You got it?"

"I got it."

"I want you to do at least five hundred catches of each kind every time you come here."

"Okay."

"I'm not even going to check and see if you did it. If you do it, I will know; and if you don't do it . . . I'll know that, too."

So I would trek to Garfield every chance I got. I must have spent several hundred hours there over the next several years. I can close my eyes and still see the playground, still see every brick in the wall. Only then, they weren't bricks. They were Brooks Robinson, Pete Rose, Rod Carew, and a host of the Major League's finest—and they were all trying to smack a hit past me. I can't tell you how many times they succeeded, and I had to chase my errant Spalding all the way to the edge of the schoolyard. But chase it I did: a lot at first, less so as the months and years passed. My ever-present internal play-by-play voice adding drama to the mundane and the occasional wink Tom would give me in an actual game kept me as riveted as any modern video game.

Several years and several thousand practice moments later, my moment arrived. We were at a company picnic for my father's company, and he, being the general manager of the facility, was playing host. Dad worked in the transportation industry, in the height of its contentious union versus management era, and here we were at the company picnic. As you might imagine, it was "us versus them" and not a small amount of machismo in the air. I was sent to right field, generally the safest place to plant me since there were few left-handed batters and no opposite field hitters in pick-up games of this sort.

It was late in the game, perhaps not the two-man out, bottom of the ninth scenario, but a reasonable facsimile. A solid hit by the opposing batter and the game would be lost for our side. I watched with eagerness: Tom was playing short because he could cover short, second, and third from that vantage point; Kevin was playing center because his speed and throwing arm basically meant he was playing the entire outfield—so I was generally comfortable that this game was well in hand. The batter fouled off several pitches in a row, and they limped off his bat with such a lack of "pop" that I had imagined he would soon yield a weak grounder that Tom would field and it'd be lights out.

I can still hear the clank of the aluminum bat. I can still see the trajectory of the softball down the first baseline. I don't remember thinking I should react—my first (and only) experience with muscle memory—I just ran in the direction of the ball's flight. There'd be no way for Kevin to bail me out; this ball was hugging the line all the way. I got underneath it, but had misjudged the distance. I knew this because I had done the same at Garfield Elementary so many times before.

More from sheer desperation than athletic instinct, I lunged backward, extending my glove out as far as I could—and made the catch of a lifetime. I stumbled, hit the ground, did a backward somersault, all of which added nicely to the drama of the moment, and came to my feet with the ball in my glove. By this time, Kevin had made his way to me, picked up my ball cap, smacked it on his thigh to shake the grass out of it, and placed it back atop my head. We trotted in together from the outfield to the cheers of our team and my dad calling me "The Say Hey Kid," a deference to Say Hey Willie Mays and his over-the-shoulder catch in the 1954 World Series.

While I hadn't won the World Series, I had gotten to

enjoy a pcak moment—a moment born of countless hours of imagining it.

We cast ourselves in the roles of our heroes, legends all, who rose mightily to every challenge—dauntless, indefatigable, Spartan stalwarts who conquered demons of doubt, gently doffed the caps—and stoically went off to face and conquer the next obstacle in their path.

No matter how insurmountable the obstacles, how long the odds, how dire the straits, we envisioned ourselves pulling through, as they had, and rising into the rarefied air of a clutch performance.

For some the notion of crafting your future through the power of your visualization of it is naught but nonsense, the endless march of hyperbole, the fruitless exercise of imagination. For me, it's something all together different. It's the underscoring of the grandeur of life; it's a celebration of the richness we are privileged to experience; it's transforming the ordinary to the extraordinary in a way that puts celebrating life into the muscle memory of our thoughts so when moments that cause for celebration arrive we celebrate.

It's all about how you look . . . at the crabapples.

Sand Scripts

Milestones
are most often preceded
by miles of stone.

The Best of Infinity

Always give yourself a chance to win

I think every kid who ever played neighborhood games learned the meaning of infinity by their powers of deduction, more than by any effort to look it up in the dictionary or wait until your junior high speller had you wondering what the word meant. Usually, you were introduced to it in the throes of an argument—like the one I witnessed between the Paressi brothers: Steve, the older (and more academically challenged), and Richie, the younger, my neighborhood best buddy. Only eighteen months apart, the two were constantly at odds. They were arguing, in this instance, the ubiquitous argument of athletic acumen which unfolded endlessly in neighborhoods back in the day.

"You fat little turd. I'm twice as fast as you."

"Are not."

"I can throw twice as far."

"So what?"

"And I'm ten times stronger than you!"

Having to yield to the obvious, Steve being far more athletically accomplished than the more cerebral Richie, Richie turned to his trusted mental muscles to return a barb.

"Yeah, and you're ten times uglier, too."

Flustered by the change of direction in what had now become a battle of wits, Steve blurted back, "You're a hundred times uglier!"

"Than you?"

"Yeah! You're a hundred times uglier than me."

"So you are admitting that you are ugly?"

Even more flustered than just a moment ago, Steve scanned his mental terrain for the light of a retort. When it came, he leaned in toward Dave like a pitcher about to throw the strike that ends the game.

"I'm admitting that I am stronger, faster, and better looking than you—times *infinity.*"

I was ten years old at the time, and I didn't need to search through the family's *Funk & Wagnalls* to understand that infinity meant forever. If only adult arguments could end as neatly as those in childhood—you invoked the infinity clause in a neighborhood and that argument was finito.

The concept *best of* usually landed on the consciousness of a young sandlotter the first time he got the better of someone who either didn't want to face the consequence of the lost contest or thought himself so superior to his underling that clearly "luck" had carried the moment and they demanded a chance to reverse the outcome. I first witnessed it as the proposed resolution to an argument my older brothers were having.

"Your turn to take out the trash."

"Is not. I did it last week."

"It's gotta be out there before the old man gets home."

"So take it out."

"Bite me. You take it out."

They, like so many siblings or mates, had argued so many times in their lives that they instantly knew the arbitrator of luck was the only way to settle the disagreement. They assumed the position and one of them would call the contest of choice.

"I got odds."

So they'd face off to throw fingers, and depending on the total fingers thrust to a common middle ground, you won or lost the contest.

"Four—that's even sucker. Enjoy the trash."

And then came the counter parry.

"Best two out of three . . ."

The whole *best of* concept is as brilliant as it is simple. It's the notion that the contest is too important to be left to anything as fickle as a lucky shot, chance swing, or once-in-a-million-you-could-never-repeat-it-therefore-it-is-not-valid shot. *Best of* sets the standard that in order to be declared "best," you must vex your opponent over a course of contests in which the notion of luck can be effectively negated by the need to achieve repeated demonstrations of superior ability.

The crowning championship series of most sports is a *best of* format. One summer we chose sides for our street-baseball game, and the first several games were so close in score and brilliantly contested that we decided right then to have a best-of-seven-sevens championship, meaning you had to win four seven-game series to be declared the champion.

I am proud to say my younger brother, Tim, got his orientation to the concept in a very traditional way. Being his older brother by four years, and he entering sandlot play at a time when our older brothers were already inducted in the neighborhood hall of fame, it was left to me to oversee his tutelage in the ways of neighborhood games. I remember being proud of myself when I, in an effort to present him a challenge he could put his teeth into, spotted him twelve points in a one-on-one game of basketball we would play to twenty.

When he won the game twenty to four, he started celebrating and cackling about his victory. So I went into neighborhood loser mode.

"What are you doing?"

"I'm celebrating! I kicked your butt. I am the champion."

"Give me a break. You're not champion until you win two out of three. Everyone knows that. How could you not know that? And besides, I spotted you twelve points because I was bored."

"Then let's play again—no points this time."

"Deal."

When he won that contest twenty to fourteen, he really started to celebrate.

"What are you doing now?"

"That's it. I won two out of three, like you said."

"Oh . . . and you thought I meant two out of three games; I meant two out of three series of two out of three games. I keep forgetting what a little kid you are and how I have to explain everything."

I kept the dance alive for a few hours, always thinking I'd find a way to win, and then I'd be able to explain to our older brothers that I had been toying with him the whole time, you know, building his confidence, working on my left hand shots—anything to explain how I could have ended up on the short end of so many games.

Ultimately . . . I ran out of dodges and Tim won the final game of the final stall I could throw in the mix. When he started celebrating like a seven year old on Christmas, I became very upset, because while he was seven at the time, *clearly* it was not Christmas.

I issued a dauntless challenge, "Okay, you won this go-round, but I challenge you to the *Best of Infinity!*"

Having no clue what it meant, Timmy accepted the challenge, and I deftly forestalled the conclusion that my younger brother was by far and away the superior athlete to me, his older brother, because the contest has no definable endpoint. Though he currently leads the lifetime series 1174 to 14, he cannot declare himself the victor.

I still utter the phrase to myself when I am on the perceived short side of a situation. To me, it celebrates persistence. It's the principle that if you just give me long enough, I will find a way to win. At the very least, I'll find a way to avoid losing.

"Best of Infinity" . . . always gives us a chance to win.

Sand Scripts

Never allow
a concept so arbitrary
as time
to end
your pursuit of
your goal.

The One-Point Difference

One coach's perspective becomes a gold standard of accomplishment

I once played for a coach who did not believe in "moral victories." Moral victory is an interesting concept—it's the notion that you basically had no chance of winning but comported yourself well enough in your effort to preserve dignity in defeat, nay, even to claim victory in spite of the loss. The concept held no water for Marty Stillwater, our junior varsity basketball coach in high school.

He had a chart in his office that succinctly outlined his philosophy:

Lose by 13 or more—you lost to a better team

Lose by 7–12 points—they executed better than you; they wanted it more

Lose by 2–6 points—it's the coach's fault

Lose by 1—you didn't have the heart to win

"You gotta have *heart* fellas," he would chide us as we ran suicide after suicide drill. "You gotta have *heart* . . ." his index finger thumping his chest.

Now his philosophy may seem harsh, but you had to hear the depth of his passion in order to embrace his philosophy. He truly believed in the power of an individual's will, and when aligned with a group of like-minded folk, such as teammates who had honed their will, victory could be expected.

"Listen fellas,"—fellas was his brand name for us, and he's the only person I ever encountered who could say fellas a thousand times a practice and you still felt like he was speaking directly to you—"trust me when I lay this out for you. If we get beat by a dozen or more, then the team we played was consistently better than us. They ran the floor, rebounded, hustled, and converted opportunities. That's a time when you take your lumps and you move on.

"You lose by seven to eleven points, you oughta be mad at yourselves. Seven points? What is that—three baskets and a free throw? C'mon, you're going to tell me you're okay with that? We take, what, sixty to seventy shots a game, and you're okay with three shots being the difference? C'mon fellas, you gotta have *heart.* You gotta look inside yourself and decide what you're okay with when it comes to winning and losing games 'cause you'll take that into the rest of your life; I promise you you will. People say it's not about winning, and I will tell you—yes it is. And do you wanna know why? Because winning means you had discipline, you prepared, you paid attention to detail, you put it all out there—you played from the heart.

"We lose any games by two to six points and that's on me. All that means is I didn't manage the game clock right, didn't make the right subs, didn't call the right time outs, and didn't coach you guys into a position to win.

"Now here's the thing: people look at one-point losses and they say to the losing team, 'great game,' 'good try,' some nonsense about a moral victory. Let me tell ya, fellas, living right, no drugs, no drinking—those are moral victories. Losing a basketball game by one point—that's a loss due to lack of heart."

There'd be grumblings in the room at this point.

"Be clear about this; be clear about this . . . you have to respect yourself enough not to lose by one point. If you're within one point of a victory, it means you *did* prepare; you *did* have discipline; you *did* pay attention to detail. Now you're in position to win—and you gotta find a way to win because

158

the win is the world saluting your valor, your courage, your determination, and you want that for yourself. You gotta want that for yourself. You gotta have heart. The one point is not the digit on the scoreboard; the one point is—did you respect yourself enough to win?"

His words, "play from the heart" have remained with me my entire life. His legacy was one of perspective, a perspective of preserving one's dignity through relentless effort, discipline, determination, candor, frankness, leave-it-on-the-line, and find-a-way to accomplish your goal.

I remember over the course of my seven-year odyssey to become published, receiving the most glowing rejections— two and three page letters detailing the most talent-laden parts of my manuscript, but ultimately alluding to its shortcoming and failure to gain acceptance. Every time I held one of those letters in my hands, tempted to console myself that I had come close, tempted to claim the moral victory—it was the voice of Marty Stillwater in my mind that goaded me to try again.

"You gotta ask yourself, was there something more I could have done to put myself in position to win? Did I leave it all on the floor? You gotta play from the heart, Danny; you gotta play from the heart."

People decry the emphasis on sports, but I will tell you, my experiences in sports shaped a great deal of my approach to life. I learned to honor my spirit by applying discipline, determination, attention to detail, valor, courage, and determination.

The one-point difference makes all the difference.

Sand Scripts

When the heart
carries the body
beyond what it thought
it could endure,
victory is
already in hand.

Legacy

Time for Dinner

Danny Blue Shoes

The Touchdown Trees

Legacy

Life is a gift, and if we agree to accept it,
we must contribute in return.
When we fail to contribute,
we fail to adequately answer
why we are here.
—*Albert Einstein*

I love the concept of leaving a legacy (partly because that's how I *got into college*, being the legacy of two older, academically successful siblings) and partly because the notion of giving was ingrained into my psyche both by my father's words and his actions. Not lectured onto my consciousness, but left there like a garden. My dad loved to give to others, and when you joined him on one of his clandestine charitable acts, you felt alive, excited, and purposeful. My dad lived by the notion "you can never pay back, but never miss a chance to pay forward." I think he took every act of kindness, charity, or opportunity given to him, doubled it, and gave it to others.

Perhaps it was because of this that "legacy" for me has always been more about example than words.

It's the reason my recollections of neighborhood games center on memories of older, storied neighborhood players choosing *me* for their team; of my older brothers taking pains to ensure everyone felt they were *important* to the games; of little Joey Casey being afforded the chance to be the hero by hitting a "walk-off" home run; of finding ourselves in the dark spots of relationships—when opposing wants and points of view seem irreconcilable—only to find the peace and light of respectful compromise.

We mattered to each other. Something in the circumstances of our scarcity created abundance. The genius of our neighborhood games was that they created value one could only experience by giving it to another.

After all, you can't play tag . . . alone.

Time for Dinner

The one-time bane of our neighborhood games becomes the endowment of a generation

We could set our watches by it.

We set our stomachs to it.

We realized early on we may as well set our faces *for* it, because it was as unalterable as the sun's movement across the sky.

Dinner.

The dinner bell (one family actually used one), call, or whistle was the game's irrevocable final buzzer, and not many of us gave our parents cause to call twice.

The Marshalls were first to commence eventide sup: Donny was always summoned at 5:05 to be washed and ready for the 5:15 feast; I was next, our family setting spoon to dish at 5:30; the Paressis converged on their daily feast at 6:00 p.m. sharp.

The exactness of family dinner in our day was in context to both the prevailing mores of the moment and what would today be perceived as the paucity of "modern conveniences." Families ate dinner together; it was a cultural value held in place by the absence of demands on a family's time once the afternoon sun met the rising horizon at dusk. There were no microwaves to allow one to "zap" together a quick dinner, no dishwashers to precipitate a speedy clean up of a zapped dinner, and usually only one bathroom per capita—so the

165

evening routine needed to proceed with a certain measured exactness if everyone was to arrive at bed time fed, washed, and scrubbed, as it were.

Many a day we'd file in from school through the back porch where we dispensed of our shoes, coats, and any notes from school we didn't want Mom and Dad to read, enter through the inside backdoor to be greeted by the sights, sounds, and smells of Mom preparing the evening's dinner. I remember kettles of simmering soups and stews, steam rising above their openings and tantalizing our famished bellies. We were allowed a piece of fruit for a snack, juice or milk to drink—and that was all. The simple fact that we didn't have snack foods on hand not withstanding (a treat for us was a piece of white bread covered in butter with sugar sprinkled on top), my mother lived by the adage that "hunger is the best cook."

She was the unprecedented virtuoso of yielding a lot from a little . . . but will tell you she didn't do anything differently from most moms of the era and with some degree of humility will tell you the miracle of the loaves and fishes happened on a regular basis at our house. In the early days of my father's working career job changes, company closings, layoffs, and another child born seven years in a row meant "creativity" was required in the kitchen if the family was to remain well fed. My favorite of her inventions was her habit of adding a few drops of food coloring to water and convincing us it was Kool-Aid. Having never tasted the authentic mixture, my older siblings were enormously content with the faux-aid and rather enjoyed the variety of "flavors" at their ready each and every day.

How does one manage meal time for a brood of ten, four of whom brought to the table the ravishing hunger of boys in search of manhood, and one, who, having climbed that summit, was fond of feasting on the fruits of his labors? The answer would be: with precision that would make a military mess hall proud.

My mother would prepare ten pounds of potatoes for a single meal. We consumed milk in gallons, not glasses, so Mom would buy milk and cut it by half, using something called "powdered milk," to increase the yield of the conventional gallon. I recall carrying in groceries took several of us to do and lasted forty-five minutes or more because we would have to run loads of food out to the one strategic purchase my parents had allowed themselves—a full-size freezer we kept in our garage. It came in handy when food went on sale. Many was the time my mom bought forty loaves of bread when the local A&P sold them ten for a dollar.

Sounds like soup kitchen proportions, doesn't it? And yet, those loaves didn't last a month at our house. With Dad working twelve-hour shifts as a dock foreman, our family's daily sandwich count stood at eighteen. That's a loaf of bread per day—just for lunches.

My sisters were in charge of packing our lunches, and I vividly remember coming down for breakfast on school mornings and seeing one of them making the standard daily fair: peanut butter and jelly sandwiches for eight, with me and my brothers snagging two sandwiches each. Accompanying the lunches were two sandwich cookies, or on bonus days, a handful of chocolate chip or oatmeal cookies one of my sisters had made the night before. It was tough to sit in the cafeteria day after day, reaching in the bag to pull out the PB&J as my classmates discovered exotic lunch selections like deviled ham, deli-style sandwiches, Fritos, and Ho Hos.

The rest of the culinary calendar moved with similar exactness, allowing for bulk purchase of staples on sale. Daily breakfast was always hot and varied between oatmeal, Cream of Wheat, or Coco Wheat, with a biscuit or bread of some kind added. Dinners cycled through a menu that to most sounds rigid and stoic, but was for us yet another source of something we could depend upon.

Mondays were Johnny Marzetti nights.

Tuesdays were Salisbury steak.

Wednesdays were spaghetti du jour, sometime with meatballs, sometime with spam, sometimes meatless, and sometimes courtesy of Franco American.

Thursdays were meatloaf nights.

Fridays were casseroles or some variety of hash, save for Lent when it was always tuna casserole that was served.

Saturdays were hot dogs and beans.

Sundays were reserved for pot roast, oven brown potatoes, and carrots.

The weeks unfolded with sameness, but by the time a particular day of the week came back around, be in conditioning or not, we were usually looking forward to the selection of the day. Then, too, it was not without variation. Depending on the A&P's special of the week, or a seasonal harvest, we'd find dishes like stuffed peppers, zucchini casserole, pigs-in-a-blanket, or open-faced roast beef sandwiches awaiting us at dinnertime. It was precisely the sameness of our family dinners that allowed variation from the standards to be considered such enormous treats—like the occasional Friday night in lent when Mom would serve breakfast foods for dinner.

I don't recall a single time when all ten of us ate out together at a restaurant. I can tell you now, though, it wouldn't have been nearly as much fun as eating together at home. When we moved as one in public, we moved with the awareness that our actions were under the watchful eyes of our parents, whose expectation of our behavior literally allowed for zero wiggle room.

At home, we gathered around our family dinner table like the cast and crew of a long-standing, wildly successfully sitcom. We all had character roles in which we were comfortable enough to improvise scenes and dialogue with great spontaneity while still maintaining the semblance of order needed to keep the meal moving forward.

None of us dared miss evening dinner. We convened at

the table and immediately sat in age order around it, Mom and Dad occupying the places of honor at either end of the table. Dinner began with each of us telling something about our day. Dad, ever the man of order, matched up needs or challenges with experience. If someone was struggling in math, someone else was named tutor. If someone was struggling socially, someone else offered advice. If any of us felt threatened in any way, Tom or Kevin instinctively took note and somehow those issues were reported as resolved within the next few meal times. After the daily reports, and as time went on, the restrictions on speaking during dinner loosened a bit and the rapier wit and repartee was as delectable as the food being served.

"Danny, quit picking your nose."

"I'm not picking my nose."

"You pick your nose so often your fingernails are green."

"Has anyone seen my green blouse?"

"Who stars in it?"

"Boy, I'll say Mr. Green is a louse. He assigned us the first five chapters of *Grapes of Wrath* by tomorrow."

"Don't sweat it. He does that every semester to scare kids into starting the book. He never checks if you actually read it. It's not like Sr. Loretta—you ain't go getta no—Grace."

"Tell me about it. She not only makes you write summaries of the chapters she assigned, but you have to diagram the sentences in the summary!"

"I can still hear her shrill voice, 'Devil's in the details!'"

"Yet another reason to avoid details . . ." Tom said with a mockingly profound nodding of his head, followed by my father's bemused shaking of his.

"How old *were* you going to be on your next birthday?"

My favorite dinner memories revolved around guests. We were a prime time show and we enjoyed it, but it was fun to see the dynamic playing out to an audience. Siblings having friends over were the best—we let loose with a flurry of banter that scared a few, surprised others, but usually entertained most. The dinners that weren't as fun happened when more formal guests gathered with us. Usually word would spread through the siblings before dinner, warnings about behaviors and menu item restrictions.

"Don't take any meat; there's only enough for the adults and guests."

So you'd be sitting there while they passed these platters of breaded veal cutlets so close to your nose, one wrong move and you'd have breadcrumbs in your nostrils. You didn't dare take one, even when offered.

"Would you like some veal cutlets, Danny?"

"No, no thank you."

"Well, alright honey, but eat all your lima beans and peas."

Then came the spirit crusher, the dagger in the heart of obedience. As the main course dishes were cleared away, Mom would appear from the kitchen with a seven layer chocolate cake with chocolate icing and declare, "Dessert for those who ate their meat with dinner. . . ."

They say the sense of smell is most closely connected to memory. That may be why every time I smell chili cooking on a winter's afternoon or pick up the smell of peppers baking in the fall . . . or catch the unmistakable aroma of kielbasa and sauerkraut, I am transported back to the cocoon-like security and sanctity of our family dinner table. Looking back at that time from the vantage point of our frenzied, hurried, and at times harried lives, who could have foretold that the one-time bane of our existence, the moment that caused the game of the day to cease, would now stand as the legacy of our generation?

That legacy lies in the simple fact that we took . . . time for dinner.

Sand Scripts

The greatest treasure
families can store up—
is the richness
of time spent
together.

Danny Blue Shoes

The enduring legacy of . . . your nickname

Nothing signified your legacy in neighborhood play quite like your nickname. Nicknames were the shorthand code for identifying your most redeeming, or in some cases, your most damning quality. You always wanted to be known as "Danny the Clutch" and not "Danny the Klutz." The history of modern pop and sports culture, from the turn of the twentieth century on, has had a love affair with the nickname.

Joltin' Joe DiMaggio

Shoeless Joe Jackson

Joe Willie White Shoes Namath

Pistol Pete Maravich

Say Hey Willie Mays

Kenny the Snake Stabler . . . and on goes the list.

You always wanted to have earned your nickname rather than have it stuck to you because of some random act or physical attribute you couldn't control. If you don't think nicknames are impactful, ask Stevie "The Schnoz" Cerellio how he feels about being forever known by the size of his nose.

Nicknames were a staple of our life at home, as well. Probably because forty years after he'd left the streets of the Bronx, my dad could still role off the nicknames of guys he grew up with and tell you why they were so named.

He had awe and reverence in his eye when he'd tell you

the exploits of "Ironhead" McGee, famous for head butting opponents into oblivion, or "Dutch" Johnson, a tough-minded Norwegian who used to put newspaper inside his thin coat to keep warm in the winter because his family couldn't afford new clothing. There was "Big Hands" Flannery, whose hands were so massive they made a basketball seem like an orange when he held it. We also came to know our Uncle Jim, Dad's older brother, as "Tank" Porter, a kid so tough he played tackle football wearing only a knit cap.

He'd have a glint of humor when he remembered the names they'd given the less gifted and athletically accomplished among themselves. "Stone Hands" Strastinsky "couldn't catch a cold"; "Hard Luck" Hannahan—every bad bounce of a ball found this guy; and "Goose-Egg" Grady. "He played in almost every contest, game, or round of skill I can remember and never scored a point."

Dad was the originator of the nicknames my brothers enjoyed. My eldest brother, Tom, sharing my father's given name, was called by his middle name, "Shane," most of our childhood. When I came to understand it was given him after one of my father's favorite westerns, I thought it was especially cool, rugged, and steely. Like Tom.

My next eldest brother, Kevin, had a maverick streak that got him tagged with the moniker of Dad's personal hero, John Wayne—"Duke."

I got several cool versions of my given name, being called Danny Joe, Dan'l, and Dano depending on if *Daniel Boone* or *Hawaii Five-O* was being watched.

In the neighborhood it was different. In the neighborhood your nickname came either from your physical skills (or lack thereof) or some facet of your persona.

The conferring of a nickname in neighborhood play may as well have been a christening, because that would be your given name the rest of your natural life. Keenly aware of this, I set about consciously cultivating my brand. I figured if I could coin one for myself before someone else did, it would reflect more my persona than my athletic ability.

I chose "The Bubblegum Kid."

I don't remember the major leaguer I tried to pattern myself after, but somewhere along the line I had seen a highlight of a baseball player popping a bubble as he shot the gap at short, scooped up a certain base hit, and turned a double play, popping another bubble to signify the triumph. The minute I saw him, I knew I wanted that to be my signature move. In part because *Butch Cassidy and the Sundance Kid* were popular at the time, and in part to dispel the notion I couldn't walk and chew gum at the same time.

Skanking every stray piece of gum I could find, I first went to work on my popping technique. I wanted the ability to "snap, crackle, and pop" the gum, to blow the effortless bubble that signified my cool.

It took months before I felt confident enough in my chewing and bubble gum blowing ability to combine the gum with my game.

The first time I tried to combine blowing a bubble with swinging the bat, my older brother, Tom, had to initiate the Heimlich maneuver on me—I think, actually, *before* the maneuver had been invented.

Persistent, I tried it again on a high-fly hit to me in left field. I blew the bubble, placed my free hand under my glove hand, the ball smacked into my mitt so hard it pushed my wristband into my bubblegum, and it took me a week to separate the two.

Dauntlessly, I forged onward. I kept up my bubblegum blowing practice, shortened my bubble size, focused more on cracking the gum, and persisted in my practice of baseball.

I was playing third in an actual little league game. I had a few put outs and was in general feeling pretty good about myself that day. In the fifth inning, a shot came my way and I felt so good I decided to go for my idol's move. I blew a bubble, laid the glove to the ground—and that's pretty much all I remember. When I came to, the coach and a few players were standing over me, some laughing, some just shaking their heads.

What really hurt was the welt on my head that was bigger than any bubble I'd ever blown.

~~The Bubblegum Kid.~~

Danny "Strawberry Head" Porter.

I begged God to let me make the eighth-grade basketball team. All my buddies were on the team and all the girls we had crushes on were cheerleaders. To not be part of this would have been certain social Armageddon.

After I made the team (Brian Urdash broke his foot skateboarding, leaving one spot vacant), I begged for God to move my parents' heart to get me a new pair of Chuck Taylor Converse All-Stars, the shoe of champions in my day. It was also one of the first years Converse had come out with colors to match the local school's colors.

Miraculously, Dad came through the door one night with a box of Converse under one arm. He, a Depression-era kid who got a new pair of shoes any time his brother's hand-me-down shoes were too sole bare to wear, had gotten me a new pair of shoes, in the middle of the school year, just for making the team.

I'll never forget the conflict I felt opening the box. The shoes were Carolina blue.

Our uniforms were burgundy with gold trim.

I was sitting on the edge of my bed, staring at my shoes, when my brother, Tom, came by. He looked at the shoes, looked at me, looked back at the shoes . . . and smiled.

"You'd have to be *really* good to wear those shoes with that uniform and get away with it."

"I know," I forlornly replied.

"So . . ." he said, needing to draw the joke to its punch

line, "what are *you* going to do?"

I had no idea.

I remember as kids we tried everything we could to create larger-than-life personas for ourselves. We wanted something to be a signature of who we were. From the way we wore our socks, to the way we wore our hats—something had to be distinct and unique to us.

Baby blue sneaks were not what I had in mind for my signature look. Too bad Shoeless Joe Jackson already claimed that great nickname and motif.

I became known as "Knees" that year because all you ever saw of me when you looked down the bench was knees. I had my feet tucked away so tightly that if the coach ever put me in a game (thank God *that* never happened), our trainer would have had to perform minor surgery to get my feet free.

It wasn't until thirty years later when my brother ran into my old eighth-grade basketball coach, Coach Tambouro, that the blue shoes got the proper perspective for me.

"How's Danny Blue Shoes doin'?"

Tom proceeded to catch up Coach on my exploits, including my journey to become published.

Coach Tambouro shook his head. "I'm not surprised; that boy was all heart. He had no business being on the basketball court, and yet, there was no way I was going to keep him off it."

Tom said Coach Tambouro smiled and added, "But . . . those shoes . . ."

Here's the thing, though, the fates had it in for me from the get-go when it came to this whole notion of nicknames and the legacies they create for you. Our eighth-grade basketball team went undefeated that year. We won every regular season game, entered the tournament, and proceeded to whip the entire field. However, it was hard for us to feel tough, macho, and champion-like—because of the name of our school.

I went to Catholic grade school, so of course we played

in the CYO (Catholic Youth Organization) league. We played against schools named for the faith's toughest saints, their strongest icons.

We played against:

St. Dominic Dominators

St. Michael the Archangel Avengers

St. Ignatius Crusaders

St. Daniel Lions

The name of our school?

Our Lady of Perpetual Sorrow.

Our nickname?

The Mourners.

Strikes fear in the hearts of opponents, don't you think? You should have heard our cheer:

Oh yeah! Oh Wow!

You think you're something now!

But wait! You'll see!

You'll be sad for eternity!

Sand Scripts

Your legacy
to me
is how you were
always present
in my life.
Because you were
there then,
you are here now,
and you always will be
with me.

Touchdown Trees

Stand for something

There are no bald spots in my father's lawn. Grass has filled in the dirt patches that had once been home plate, the pitcher's mound, and the end zone. It was as if time had acted like the hand of one brushing suede one way to darken it, the opposite way to lighten it. We had lightened the yard, pushing its grass down in the direction of our play, and now time had pushed it back the other way to darken it. One could shoot a laser across the lawn and every blade of grass would measure the same height. The shrubs are trimmed to perfection; neat mulch beds adorn all the trees. The ornamental orange tree is perfectly proportioned because no one stands by it at third base and picks off the leaves until half of it looked blighted.

And yet, to me, the yard had never looked sadder.

"When you gonna do somethin' about that yard, Porter? You're dragging down the property values on the whole block!"

"I'm raisin' kids, Wilson, not grass."

The comment, though perhaps not original, was my father's signature response to anyone who inquired how he tolerated the appearance of every yard of every home he owned. A stickler for cleanliness inside our home and even in the garage, a man notorious for impeccable order in his business—it must have seemed an anomaly to anyone who knew him that the yards of his homes looked as badly as ours

181

did.

We wreaked havoc on them, I am here to confess. Trudging up and down their boundaries, standing on them tossing balls for hours, the shuffling of our feet to throw and catch like sandpaper to porcelain, we were to his urban landscape what the buffalo were to the plains. In all that time, though, I never heard Dad utter a complaint or regret about the state of the yard. Oh sure, he'd have us out there every spring for a yard reclamation project, but it only lasted until the first run of good weather after opening day, and then we'd promptly undo all the progress nature had made.

Perhaps the journey of his own youth, the son of Irish immigrants, his father a journeyman landlord, moving from building to building, and Dad playing ball in alleyways and sometimes rooftops, made him proud of the opportunities we had to play right there on the plots of land that were his yards.

When my father passed away, in the hustle and hurry of greeting relatives and friends, of sharing memories, celebrating his life, and absorbing our sadness, I found a pause to walk out onto his front yard. It was then I realized three generations of youth had romped across it. First my brothers and me; and then, when we had grown, Dad let the neighborhood kids have unlimited access to it because it offered the longest expanse of level ground in the neighborhood. Finally, his grandchildren were granted use of it, and they, too, slid and frolicked at the expense of the bluegrass and arbor vitas. I stood looking across it and back across all the years of all the games it had hosted. Now it stood as silent, sullen, and abandoned as his beloved Ebbets Field must have been when the Brooklyn Dodgers left for Los Angeles.

Only the Touchdown Trees remained.

The Touchdown Trees were two perfectly shaped, perfectly spaced ash trees that marked one of the end zones. They were the kind of trees companies would choose as a logo, that's how perfectly their canopies rose above the yard. I remember diving for glory many a time, looking up under their foliage to see their branches signaling a touchdown.

As I stood there, remembering all he had been and given us, those Touchdown Trees stood as sentinels to one of Dad's legacies, guardians of his own field of dreams.

"Let the kids play. . . ."

Sand Scripts

The best legacies
are gifts of the heart,
the sort of which
inspire the recipients
to leave a legacy

Epilogue

Pass It On

The Sandlot Creed

To fall and to rise, to fall again and to rise again . . . I learned that from my brothers and from our neighborhood ways. I learned what it meant to earn respect simply by your unwillingness to quit. I learned that determination, courage, and persistence are not unending continuums within those we call our heroes; there are moments of morbid doubt, of lightless despair, of the certainty that balance is forevermore lost; and I learned that what is important is to remember these are but "moments" and that "players" always play again, they always find a way, they always fill a role, and they always make a contribution.

One late August afternoon, as I was finishing a session working on this book, I emerged from my office as a man possessed by a vision of a better fate for modern youth than to have everything at their fingertips and yet no opportunities to experience and learn in the ways that we did.

So I rousted my children from the house and had them go and gather every able-bodied child from their suburban slumber. Surprisingly, within thirty minutes or so, there was a gaggle of kids in our driveway.

"Okay guys," I bellowed like a camp counselor who had had one too many mocha lattes that morning, "let's organize a game of baseball."

Silence fell upon the group.

"I play baseball at the Steiner Center on Tuesdays and

Thursdays," said Matt, his face belying his confusion. Why would he dream of playing now, here, in the middle of a Tuesday afternoon in his own neighborhood?

"Where are we going to play?" Megan wanted to know.

"My mom can drive us to the park. It's only twenty minutes away," Shelby offered.

"I don't play baseball . . ." said David. "The practices are the same time as my French lessons."

Only five minutes in and already I needed to regain control of the group. I briefly looked at my yard, remembered the endless hours of planting this beautiful blend of Kentucky Blue, rye, and turf grasses, the thousands of dollars in fertilizers, the faithful watering, the aerations . . . and announced, "We'll play in my yard."

We set up the bases, established the base paths, split the group into teams, and began to play.

Stamina and attention span they had not.

"Katie, uh, Katie—you need to look over here, honey."

"Why?"

"Well, because Shannon may hit the ball and it may come to you."

"She hasn't hit it yet. . . ."

*"And she's not likely **to** hit it, given she's holding the bat like a parasol. . . ."*

Katie's observation unleashed a torrent of "I'm bored," and "this stinks." So, recognizing the heat was getting to them, I made another valiant suggestion.

"Let's have a water war."

"Sounds stupid," Katie complained.

"A what?" Nathaniel's ears perked up. If nothing else, it sounded violent.

"A water war."

"What's that?" he persisted.

"You shouldn't call anything a war," Brianne objected, "Wars are horrible things and children's games shouldn't be called 'wars.' It's not right."

"You're right, Brianne," I stammered. "I am so sorry. Let's call it a *Splashoree.*"

"*Now* it sounds stupid," Nathaniel protested.

"Here's what we'll do," I forged ahead. "We'll keep the same teams we had in baseball and each team gets three buckets. You have fillers and chasers. You score by getting a bucket of water to hit, sorry, to "splash" on an opposing team's player."

By now I had arrived at our side yard spigot and I was filling one of my daughter's sand pails with water.

"Sounds like paint ball," said Andy.

"Yeah!" Nathaniel expediently agreed. "Let's just go play paint ball at the laser dome."

"NO!" I decried, sounding very much like I was about to take my ball and go home.

"Why not?"

"Because the idea is to have some homemade fun, right here in our neighborhood—without taking out the minivan to go spend a hundred dollars on playing games we can play right here for free."

"Well, those buckets are lousy. I'm getting my Randex 3850 super soaker with repeat action pumper and . . ."

At that point I did what any self-respecting, nurturing, guardian of the inner child everywhere adult should do when faced with a group of children who didn't want to play.

I dumped a sand bucket's worth of water on Nathaniel's head.

There was a split second of indecision as to whether he should retaliate or go home, call the family's attorney, and file a lawsuit.

He chose the first option, seizing the hose from my hand (I let him, the hose burns on my hands were purely for effect) and soaking me aplenty. The "Splashoree" was underway.

It raged on for hours through the remainder of that

summer afternoon. It took out several prize-winning hostas from our backyard, but they died for a greater cause. The kids laughed and chased one another. They organized assaults, launched salvos, retreated, and regrouped. I found the right moment and slipped away so they could continue—unaided by the stringent presence of anyone over thirteen.

As the action waned, my wife and I brought treats out on our patio. I listened as the kids were now recreating the afternoon's best moments.

"Did you see it when Andy got hit right in the face and started choking on the water that he swallowed?"

"Did you see Nick get hit in the you-know-where and then it looked like he was peeing?"

"He was peeing."

"Was not!"

Amidst the chatter, young Nathaniel looked over at me and asked, "So what else did you guys play as kids?"

If you drive through the fifteen hundred-home subdivision where I live, there among the immaculately kept yards, the fountain cherry trees, the white birch trees, the Japanese maples, the puffs of swamp grass flowing gracefully within their unlikely suburban home, you'll recognize my yard immediately. It's bordered by the obligatory Bradford pear trees, highlighted with the rare Mimosa tree we cultivated from a seedling, and filled with award-winning azaleas and dwarf lilac trees.

It also has several bald spots that serve as home plate or the end zone, depending on the season. And if you drive by, listen closely . . . that thwap you hear—it's a screen door whose spring is shouting to whoever will listen—

"Game Time!"

Sand Scripts

The Sandlot Creed

Always run another one. . . .
Don't let the game end with you. . . .
Pass it on.

About the Author

Daniel J. Porter is the published author of twenty-two books for children. He has 2.2 million books in print and has earned three national best sellers. *'Til The Streetlights Came On* is his first adult narrative nonfiction title.